NORMAN VINCENT PEALE

IN GOD
WE TRUST

A POSITIVE
FAITH for
TROUBLED
TIMES

By Norman Vincent Peale

The Amazing Results of Positive Thinking
Enthusiasm Makes the Difference
A Guide to Confident Living
Have a Great Day—Every Day
How To Be Your Best
Inspiring Messages for Daily Living
The Positive Power of Jesus Christ
The New Art of Living
Positive Imaging
Power of the Plus Factor
The Positive Principles Today
The Power of Positive Living
The Power of Positive Thinking
Sin, Sex, and Self-Control
Stay Alive All Your Life
The Tough-Minded Optimist
You Can If You Think You Can
Norman Vincent Peale's Treasury of
    Courage and Confidence
Norman Vincent Peale's Treasury of
    Joy and Enthusiasm
The True Joy of Positive Living
This Incredible Century

By Norman Vincent Peale and Smiley Blanton

The Art of Real Happiness
Faith Is the Answer

NORMAN VINCENT PEALE

IN GOD WE TRUST

A POSITIVE FAITH for TROUBLED TIMES

Publishers Since 1798

THOMAS NELSON PUBLISHERS

Nashville • Atlanta • London • Vancouver

Published in Nashville, Tennessee, by Thomas Nelson, Inc.,

Unless otherwise noted, Scripture quotations are from The Holy Bible, KING JAMES VERSION.

Library of Congress Cataloging-in-Publication Data

Peale, Norman Vincent, 1898-1993

    In God we trust : a positive faith for troubled times / Norman Vincent Peale.

    p.   cm.

    Originally published: Pawling, NY : Peale Center for Christian Living, 1994.

    Includes bibliographical references.

    ISBN 0-7852-7675-0 (hc)

    1. Christian Life.   I. Title.

BV4501.2.P3629 1995

248.4—dc20   95-16461

                                  CIP

Printed in the United States of America

2 3 4 5 6 7 - 00 99 98

CONTENTS

INTRODUCTION

Everywhere, people are asking, "What can we do about the struggles we face today? What can anyone do? Is there anything one individual can do that will make a difference in these troubled times?"

These questions are usually asked with an air of futility. The implication is that one individual is impotent, that he can do little, that he is an insignificant factor in any situation.

Fears assail us; anxieties haunt us; we become irritated and nervous. We are hit by hurricanes or floods, recessions and job layoffs. Prayer is no longer permitted in the public schools, half the adult population in the United States is illiterate, and schoolchildren carry guns and knives to school for protection. It's no wonder that many people don't know where to turn or what to do to live a decent, happy life. The people are becoming the servants of government, and the individual seems of no importance. America cannot be the great nation it was destined to be, unless we restore to it the faith in the old American principle of resourceful, resolute human beings standing as individuals.

Our fathers handed down to us a prosperous and happy country. They said, "We built this country on certain principles, see ye to it; remain faithful." But we bowed God out, and became indifferent to spiritual things. As a result, our social situation is the most confused of all time.

Nowadays, many working parents, or single-parent families, say there's no time to go to church. They are not bad people—they have just grown careless. They do not realize that they are contributing to the process of drifting away from the great vital things that are needed to sustain an individual, a family, or the nation.

But there is hope. A positive, victorious faith is available to anyone and everyone. It is available to you—the kind of faith by which you can overcome all the circumstances of this life that otherwise would defeat you. Such faith is not cheaply had, nor easily attainable. To get it, you must go deeply into religion. If you simply skim the surface of Christianity, you will get superficial results. But if you sink deeply into it and let it seep deeply into you, you will be able to overcome all the difficulties you will meet in life. It is out of deepest personal conviction that I make this statement, for there is nothing my experience has more deeply impressed upon me than that everyone of us, if he will, can have a positive faith, no matter how troubled the times are.

Humble yourself. Pray. Trust in God. Turn to Him. Go to church. Get yourself a deep faith in Jesus Christ, a positive faith that will carry you through all times, especially the troubled ones.

Now, I presume that there are people who will say that this suggestion is antiquated, old-fashioned doctrine. If so, then we've lost connection with one of the greatest truths that was ever proclaimed by man or by God—that the greatest thing anyone can do is have the experience of standing up against a devastating situation and saying with all his heart, "I can take care of this situation, with the help of Almighty God."

The first step, then, is to fill your life with a positive faith that will help you through anything. The second is to begin where you are. Don't wait for someone else to change things for you. Do it yourself.

Do the job that is at hand. Don't wait. Seize upon it. Begin at your own place and start from there.

This book was written to help guide you toward developing the type of faith that will help you overcome the kinds of problems we face as a nation, or as an individual. To do this, you must return to the basic principles of faith. Not a superficial faith, but one that goes deep into the core of your soul. Through persistence, self-knowledge, prayer, commitment, optimism, a resolute trust in God, and the building of your own personal moral strength, you can enjoy the blessings of a deeper faith, and face the difficulties of life with courage and confidence. Begin where you are. Begin now.

Norman Vincent Peale
November 20, 1993

CHAPTER 1

Keep On Keeping On

I can do all things through Christ who strengthens me.

—*Phillipians 4:13*

W HAT will you do when the going gets rough in your life, as almost inevitably it will? Do you have what it takes to handle the more difficult challenges of human existence, if the days of good fortune run out and dark, hard days begin? Sooner or later, everyone has to realize that life is indeed hard; that it is, sometimes, almost harder than one can handle. Yet it *has* to be handled.

I heard, the other day, of a man who had really hit bottom financially. He'd had a business failure, and practically everything had gone to pay off his debts. His home was up for sale. Assignment was made even of his personal belongings. Officers came, by order of the court, and took away his car, leaving him without his own transportation.

That evening, bound for home, he was standing on a street corner with the thought of hailing a taxi; but it occurred to him that he was so reduced financially that this would be an extravagance. He was unfamiliar with public transportation but, as he was standing there in deep discouragement, wondering what to do, a big truck drew up

3

to the curb and a nice-looking, friendly truck driver asked him if he would like a lift. (One marvels at the way God works sometimes. This truck driver was exactly what the bankrupt man needed at that moment, but who would have thought it would happen in this way?)

As they drove along, the businessman sensed something in this truck driver that aroused his confidence. He opened up and poured out in detail all the difficulties he faced, finding comfort in unburdening his mind in this manner.

The truck driver was, to a degree at least, a philosopher. And he said, "Well, my friend, it's too bad. That's life. It can treat you real rough." And then he used an unusual phrase: He said, "Sometimes you've got to learn how to keep on keeping on."

This, indeed, is one of the basic skills of living: knowing how to be persistent, how to keep at it, or in the trucker's phraseology, how to keep on keeping on. And everyone can learn how to do just that. The best way is to discover the truth that the way to handle some ordeal or difficulty is to keep calm, to think rationally, to meditate, and then to concentrate on the problem. Your mind is a powerful instrument. If it controls you, you'll not be victorious. But if you control it, you will be.

However, a human being, by his own unaided strength, cannot accomplish this. Something else needs to be added. The distressed man mentioned above found a wonderful dynamic thought that held him steady, and he made his way back up. This thought changed everything. And it is one of the greatest anyone can ever grasp. It is embedded in the Bible, the wisest Book ever written. And given what I know about human beings and about the Bible and about

God, I will guarantee that this thought can help anyone under any circumstance keep on keeping on. Everyone would do well to hold it in consciousness, until it absorbs into the unconsciousness, and then live completely by it. It is found in Philippians 4:13: "I can do all things through . . ." . . . myself? No. "I can do all things through Christ who strengthens me." Christ will help you keep on keeping on.

Everyone, at one time or another, suffers a crisis, or even a defeat. "You can't win them all," someone said. What, then, do you do about the challenges you don't win? What about the harsh defeats that come? Physical defeats, for example, when you have trouble with your health, when your body begins to give up on you. What do you do about pain, sorrow, suffering, and hardship? What happens when you are defeated in some objective, or in some ambition? Or when you see that some fond hope, cherished for years, is not going to be realized? What happens when life seems to flow away from you, rather than toward you; when things get mixed up and become unhappy; when you are having trouble with yourself, and trouble with everything else? What do you do?

The greatest measure of a human being isn't how he handles himself when things are going well, but how he handles himself when things are going badly, when defeat comes. The attitude a person has in defeat is a great issue in life, for it determines whether one is able to overcome difficulties and be victorious again.

I have in my library a book entitled *Success Through a Positive Mental Attitude,* by Clement Stone and Napoleon Hill. It is a good book. And in it is a story I will retell here. It is a story about two race horses.

When I was a boy, the greatest race horse in the United States was generally considered to be Man O' War. Indeed, never had there been a race horse to equal him. I saw him race once. It was superb—poetry in motion. What a magnificent animal he was! And the jockey who rode him almost seemed to be a part of the horse, so that the two moved as one. Watching Man O' War was an unforgettable sports experience, like the time, years ago, when I saw Jackie Robinson, at Ebbetts Field, steal second base, then third and, finally, home. Such experiences you never forget.

Well, at any rate, Man O' War had it all his own way for several years. Then another horse began to challenge him. And it is the story of this other horse, named John P. Grier, that is related in the book. You have never heard of John P. Grier? That is not surprising, for he had only momentary fame.

Well, this John P. Grier looked pretty good. People said, "He's a great horse. He can rival Man O' War." So they finally got the two of them in a race. They both got away cleanly at the starting post. They were even at the first quarter. They were even at the second quarter, they were even at the third quarter, they were even at the eighth pole. Then the spectators leaped to their feet, electrified. John P. Grier was edging ahead. Man O' War was facing the challenge of his life.

But the jockey sitting on top of Man O' War did some thinking. He had never hit Man O' War with a whip. The great horse always had sufficient motivation without the whip. And the jockey wondered, *Shall I hit him with the whip?* The thought came to him, *If I don't hit him, he's going to be second.* So he hit him with the whip. And this

6

startled Man O' War. He had never felt the touch of a whip before. And under the shock of it, he became a ball of fire. He surged across the finish line seven lengths ahead, still the champion.

Well, so far so good, but that is not the main point of the story. The point is what happened to John P. Grier. That race was to be his one moment of glory, but he was defeated. Now, I'm no authority on the psychology of a horse. But it must be similar to that of people, because this horse, John P. Grier, never challenged any great race horse again. Apparently, his defeat by Man O' War left him hurt inside.

Deep down, he was a soft horse. He couldn't take it. His performance after that race was weak, half-hearted, apathetic. If he had been a positive thinking horse, he would have said to himself, "I almost beat that Man O' War. Next time, I'll really take him over." But he was soft. He didn't have in him the makings of a champion. He was the victim of his weakness. He let defeat defeat him.

What are *you* going to do with defeat? Are you going to let it defeat you? Or are you going to make it a positive, creative experience from which you can extract much know-how and wisdom and from which you will gain strength to proceed? The individual who has placed at the center of his thinking the wonderful affirmation, "I can do all things through Christ" can recover from any defeat and can handle any situation.

One time, at a convention in Chicago, I talked with a man who had been awarded the honor as the leading producer of the year in his industry. This man had an outgoing personality if I ever saw one. He said to me, "I want to tell you something, Norman. I've read all the books about how to get ahead. And, believe me, I've gotten ahead. I'm now the biggest producer in the industry. And I'm on my way to realizing my great ambition."

"What is your ambition?" I asked.

"To make a couple of million dollars a year."

"Fred," I ventured to remark, "it's all right to make some money, but you don't want to make that the big ambition of your life."

"Now, don't give me any of that religious stuff," he retorted. "I'm going places."

There was something engaging about this man, although I thought he had his values mixed up. After meeting him that day, I would hear from him from time to time. And he would tell me, "I've done this big deal; I've sold this; I've accomplished this," and so forth. But then I noticed in his letters that the effervescence had begun to die down. He finally wrote me, saying, "I don't know what's wrong with me. I've messed up everything. I've made one mistake after another. I've lost a lot of money. I'm a long ways from that two million." And with an attitude of self-pity, he continued, "I'm a no-account. I don't amount to anything. I'm stupid. I'm a fool."

I decided this called for strong talking on my part. I called Fred on the telephone. "Fred, when you let disappointment and defeat get you down, you just make things that much worse for yourself." And I suggested a series of steps for him to follow:

"Number 1. Stop putting yourself down. There is a lot that is right in you. You have the same capacity you had before. Clean your mind of your failures and mistakes and start respecting yourself.

"Number 2. Stop the self-pity. Start thinking of what

you have left, instead of dwelling on what you have lost. List your assets on a sheet of paper.

"Number 3. Stop thinking about yourself all the time. You will not have a continuing flow of abundance, if your thought is only for yourself.

"Number 4." I quoted the 18th-century German poet Goethe: " 'He who has a firm will molds the world to himself.' Almighty God put a tough thing into human beings called the will. Use it.

"Number 5. Have a goal and put a timetable on it.

"Number 6. Last, but not least (in fact, it should be first): Commit your life to Jesus and then, every morning and every night, say aloud these wonderful words: 'I can do all things through Christ who strengthens me.' "

A while later, Fred called me and said, "I want you to know that I never really lived until I took Jesus Christ as my partner. He has given me new priorities, and with them new abilities and insights have come. He has shown me how to turn my defeats into victories."

Fred had constructively handled defeat. He had learned to keep on keeping on.

I think often of my long-time friend who died only recently, Gus Bering. He was the manager of a large hotel in Chicago, the Sherman House. I often stayed there. The hotel is gone now. Gus once told me a significant story that began at a barbers' convention at the Sherman House. The leading barbers of the country were there. And they decided, on the advice of their publicity department, to put on a stunt.

These enterprising barbers went down to Madison Street, which was said to be a kind of tenderloin area in Chicago, and found a derelict, the most unfortunate specimen of humanity they could possibly find.

They took him to the Sherman House, gave him a bath, a massage, a haircut, and a manicure. Then they bought him a suit of clothes of fine quality. They put on him an expensive shirt and tie, and beautiful shoes on his feet. They gave him a fine overcoat, a hat that set jauntily on the side of his head, gloves, and a walking stick.

They took his picture before and after, and put it in the paper as an example of what the barbers could do to change a man. He made quite an impression at the barbers' convention. He was living high!

Then the convention ended and everyone forgot all about this man, all except Gus. Gus saw a man transformed. He thought, "This is wonderful. I will follow through." So he said to the man, "You have been a bum, but now you are a gentleman. Would you like to remain a gentleman?"

"Oh, yes, Mr. Bering, I sure would," the man said.

"All right," said Gus. "I'm going to give you a job, right here in this hotel. You and I and God together will make a man of you. I'd like you to start work right now."

"Well, Mr. Bering," the man said, "I've got a couple of things to attend to. How would tomorrow morning at eight o'clock do?"

A shadow of doubt crossed Mr. Bering's mind, but he agreed. And, of course, at eight o'clock the next morning, the man wasn't there. And he wasn't there at eight o'clock at night. So Mr. Bering, like the Good Shepherd hunting His lost sheep, went down into the alleyways off Madison Street and he found the man. He was dead drunk, lying on some newspapers, his expensive hat off to one side, his fine clothes rumpled and soiled; this barbers' specimen of a changed man. Mr. Bering picked him up, brought him back to the hotel, and put him to bed. The next morning, he said, "Now, my friend, I'm not going to let you go. There is a man here in this hotel, a bell hop, who has been through an experience similar to yours. I want him to talk to you."

And the bell hop told the derelict, "Gus Bering picked me up as he did you. I was as you are. I found the secret of a changed life from him. I put my life in the hands of Jesus Christ and I asked Him to take me and make me over. And I really gave myself to Him. I'm only a bell hop, but I have a wife and children and a home that's paid for."

"And," Mr. Bering put in, "the love and respect of everyone on the staff, and of the guests."

The derelict looked at that bell hop and said, "Tell me what to do."

"Just say, 'I can do all things through Christ who strengthens me.'"

And it happened again. The man was changed inside. He is no model of style now, but he is clean and decent and successful and respected. What you are inwardly, determines how you can handle things outwardly. If inside you are strong, then come what may of pain, difficulty, sorrow, trouble, or defeat, you can keep on keeping on.

Consider the postage stamp. Its usefulness consists in its ability to stick to one thing til it gets there. —Josh Billings

CHAPTER 2

Find Power
In the Positive

If ye have faith as a grain of mustard seed, ye shall say unto this mountain, Remove hence to yonder place; and it shall remove: and nothing shall be impossible unto you.

—Matthew 17:20

UNDOUBTEDLY, there are people today who have within themselves astonishing power. I think that may be said of everyone, and yet we allow the smallest and most insignificant things to frustrate our power. I do not know what it is that is resting heavily on your mind, or what constitutes an obstacle in the way of your success or happiness. But I do know that it is not necessary for you to be hobbled, hampered, or defeated.

I am constantly amazed at the astonishing power that can be released in people by the simple habit of positive thinking, which is another term for faith. Anyone who becomes a great person did so because he refused to be a little person. He refused to allow obstacles to defeat him. The most inspirational thing in life is a person who has overcome obstacles and hardships.

A shining example of such a person was James L. Kraft, founder of the great Kraft Food Corporation. One gloomy evening, long ago, Mr. Kraft had his entire business in an old wagon drawn by a horse called Paddy. He made, delivered, and sold his own cheese in Chicago. He had capital of $65, his only visible asset. He was failing. He had almost wiped out his $65.

His horse was clumping over the cobblestone streets of the city that gloomy night, and this discouraged young fellow sat on the seat of the wagon. The people who today believe that the social system should be abolished simply because they have had some difficulty should remember that this social system has produced men like James L. Kraft who are never defeated by difficulties. The fault is not so much with the system, but with the people who believe they are defeated before they start.

Mr. Kraft felt defeated that night. His reins were hanging listlessly in his hands, and he asked his horse, "Paddy, what is wrong with us?" All he heard was the cloppity clop of Paddy's shoes on the pavement. "What is wrong with us, Paddy?"

In the silence, he heard a Voice, not in any magical or mysterious way, but in the way that God always speaks to people. The Voice said, "What is wrong with you and Paddy is that you are trying to do this work without God. If you will listen to Me and believe in Me, nothing shall be impossible unto you."

Mr. Kraft later told me, "I listened and I believed and I listen today and I still believe." Until the day he died, Mr. Kraft believed that if a man will listen and cooperate with God, and if he will believe, it is still a fact that "nothing shall be impossible unto him."

Are you trying to live your life without God as a partner and a close associate, one with whom you speak and in whom you believe? If so, you are doomed to difficulty after difficulty, and failure after failure. Such an attitude of life is negative and begets negative results.

But, you may say, "I've tried positive thinking, and things didn't turn out right."

Who said everything would turn out right? And what do you mean by "right"? Do you mean as you wanted? How do you know that your idea, the thing you wanted, was in harmony with God's idea? It is my humble belief that when you and I are willing to put ourselves in harmony with God's ideas, not trying stubbornly to force our own way, then things turn out right. That does not necessarily mean as we thought we wanted.

"But," you may then say, "there are positive thinkers who suffer pain."

That's right, there are. Sometimes, by the grace of God through positive thinking, pain is eliminated. I have hundreds of letters testifying to this. There are other cases where, by the inscrutable will of God, pain is not eliminated. But the individual rises above the pain until the pain no longer masters him, but he masters it; and positive thinking has worked again. It does not work by pretending that the pain is not there. Positive thinking is realistic thinking. It always sees the negative, but it doesn't dwell on the negative and nurture it, letting it dominate the mind. It keeps the negative in proper size and grows the positive big. Thus it enables countless men and women to have serenity and power—despite continuing pain.

You may say, "I have known many sick people who tried to heal themselves with positive thinking, and they have died."

That's right! Death is a part of the human experience. Everyone will die. The questions to ask are these: How did they live? How did they die? Like galley slaves, full of fear and resistance and terror? Or did they live—and die—

17

courageously, gallantly, going into eternity with that glory with which they came from God? We will all die. Positive thinking will not spare us from death. But positive thinking can help us die like great souls returning to our eternal home.

The Gospel speaks to us of the great power of faith. In the Book of Matthew, Jesus tells us that, by faith, we may cause a mountain to be moved. What a word, *mountain!* It means a tremendous obstacle. Everyone has his mountain. "If ye have faith as a grain of mustard seed, ye shall say unto this mountain, Remove hence to yonder place; and it shall remove" (see Matthew 17:20).

You may find these things hard to believe. Yes, there are lots of true things that are hard to believe. Those who are skeptical about positive thinking will cite instances where it didn't seem to get results. But what, or who, was at fault? Was it the theory itself? Was it the principles of positive thinking? Or was it the person who was using it, or who thought he was?

"If you have faith," says the most reliable document ever written, "nothing shall be impossible." And how do you release it? You release it by changing the cast of your thoughts. By practicing belief rather than disbelief. You probably go along every day affirming, "I cannot do that, I cannot do this."

"I can't." How many times a day do you say, "I cannot do it"? All you have to do is repeat that negative thought to your subconscious mind and it will become a fact, because your subconscious mind wants to believe it anyway. Then you come up with a proposition and you hopefully ask your subconscious mind, "Can I, or can't I?" Your subconscious mind will answer that you cannot do it. You have trained it to answer negatively. Your creative imagination has formed a picture of yourself as failing. As you think, so are you. You have thought yourself into a state of disbelief in yourself.

The kind of picture a person creates in his mind is extremely important. If, over a long period of time, you create in your mind the picture that you cannot, you will inevitably have a picture of yourself failing and, therefore, you will fail. You have two powers within you, creative imagination and will. You may summon your will, which will say, "I can." But your creative imagination says, "No, you cannot." In this conflict of opinion, you cannot, because your creative imagination is stronger than your will. This is true because imagination is in the realm of belief, and what you believe in your heart determines what you can or cannot do. If, over a long period of time, you believe that with the help of God you *can* overcome, you *can* achieve, then you will get a deep fundamental, unshakable, unblurable picture that you can. Then your will and your imagination flow together, and against that power nothing negative can stand.

One of the greatest American authorities on the human mind who ever lived was the philosopher William James, who said, "Believe and your belief will in time create the fact." And the essayist and poet Ralph Waldo Emerson said, "Beware of what you want, because there is a strong likelihood that you will get it." If you want some bad thing and keep forming a picture of it, you will get it. It will come to you. The whole universe will conspire to give it to you. If, on the contrary, you want some good thing, picturize it, believe it, until it becomes your real desire; for does the Bible not say if with all your heart you truly seek, you shall find? Get into your mind positive convictions about what you want to be, what you want to become, and what you want to do. And you will go far toward attaining your goal.

A friend of mine once lost his job. It was just an ordinary job. He had a wife and two children. I thought I would comfort him, so I took him out to lunch and said, "I will be glad to help you in any way I can.

"I do not need your help," he replied. "I can handle this problem." This was so refreshing that I invited him for a second lunch. I thought it was worth it.

"Who is helping you?" I asked.

"God is helping me," he replied. "There is a job for me. I can see it in my mind's eye." He gave me the exact specifications of the job he wanted.

"You have a wife and two children—how much money do you have in the bank? Have you saved any money?"

"Not much."

"Are you interviewing potential employers?"

"Yes. I see about five people a day, and I get turned down five times a day."

"Doesn't that bother you?"

"No. I realize that I have to be turned down so many times to get this job. I do not know how many times I have to be turned down. But I know if I am turned down five times a day, that is five fewer times I have to be turned down to get the job. And I will be turned down four or five times tomorrow, four or five times the next day. It may continue a month, two months, three months, but the process just eliminates them. The 'no's' are all behind me and I will get nearer to the person who will say to me, 'Yes, here's your job.' "

One day, my unemployed friend walked into an office and described to the person there the job he wanted. The man said, "The job is here waiting for you. Where have you been?"

I attended a convention not long ago to speak. The presiding officer during part of the meeting was this friend I just told you about. I asked him, "Where did you get such ideas as that, anyway?"

And this is what he said: "I got it from the Bible. It tells us if you have faith, believe in yourself and in God, and know where you want to go, and then picture it and put it in God's hands, asking if it is His will, you will get God's help and you cannot fail."

If there is still in your mind the idea that you cannot do something, the reason you do not accomplish it is because you are thinking negatively. Start believing; start having faith. And presently, you will attain results. It is not by identifying yourself with failure, but by identifying yourself with success, that success and not failure comes to us.

There is one more thing that should be said about this matter. You might read this and say that this is simply a psychological dissertation. It is not psychological at all. Who does psychology belong to anyway? To psychologists or to God? Psychology is the study of the mind, the emotions of the body and the soul—the whole man. God owns all psychology.

When you talk about psychology, you are talking about faith, religion, God, the whole man. You cannot divide psychology and religion; they are one. Religion owns them all. However, it is a curious thing about faith. In the Bible, it is pointed out that you have to forgive if you want faith to operate in your life. You have to get all sin out.

Did you commit a sin yesterday? And are you sorry for it? I hope you are sorry. Then repent and ask the Lord's forgiveness, and don't let it linger in consciousness as guilt. If it does, it will burrow down into your unconscious and will block power in your life.

Take a person who is filled with sin, wrong, and guilt. You cannot get much faith through him. If he does succeed, it is because faith has an enormous power anyway. To have a flow of this power through a personality, to release it, you must have a transformed personality. You have to get rid of hate, ill will, grudges, licentious sins, drunken sins, all these things, for they block power. Only a little power trickles through, not enough to give great strength. If you come to Christ, and ask Him to cleanse your life and take away all this guilt, it will be so astonishing the way power will then flow through. You will exclaim, "I never lived until this minute!"

Do you remember the story of Joan of Arc? I recall seeing the motion picture years ago. As you may recall, Joan of Arc was a country girl who heard voices. God wanted to whisper to everyone, but he could not get anyone else to listen. So He went to a little village and found a country girl who was so good and pure that she was able to listen. She did not know anything about leading an army; she did not know anything about statecraft. She knew nothing except household tasks around the kitchen. But she was a good girl, and she was akin to God, so she could understand God. He whispered to her, saying, "You lead the armies of France against the invaders and you will drive them out."

She said, "Lord, I do not know anything about leading armies; I have never met the King. I do not know anyone." The movie describes how people finally listened to her. She first set out to see the old warlords, saying, "I come to bring you God's sword."

They said, "Who are you, girl? Go back to your pots and pans. You do not know anything about war."

"I come with God's bright and shining sword and, by faith, will drive out the invaders."

They ridiculed her. During her travels, she heard the soldiers swearing and saw their immorality, their gambling, and their drunkenness.

She said, "God could never do anything with an army like this." So she returned to the generals and said, "You have to tell those soldiers not to swear anymore."

They laughed and replied, "Did you ever hear of soldiers who did not swear? Do you think we are going to issue an order like that?"

She said, "I will tell them." She was marvelous as she stood before those rough men and wicked women, a lovely girl with a light of faith on her face. She said to them, "If you will yield yourselves to God and go to the church and get cleansed, then Almighty God will send a great influx of faith to you. And though we are outnumbered ten to one, we will drive the invaders from the shores of France."

And they did. They stormed the walls and, led by this marvelous figure, they won. As you watch this movie, deep down in your heart, you know that what happened is a fact. You feel a deep inner conviction that if you can rid yourself of all forms of negativism and sin you, too, can storm any wall. So form in your mind a picture of yourself believing, achieving, what God wants you to do and to be. Cleanse yourself so that His power may get through you. I do not know whether I have convinced you or not. If I have not, it is too bad; if I have, I am glad. But whether I have or not, I am telling you the truth: No matter what obstacles are before you, if you will cleanse yourself and learn to believe, it will be absolutely astonishing and amazing what your positive thinking can attain.

Throw back the shoulders, let the heart sing, let the eyes flash, let the mind be lifted up, look upward and say to yourself, "Through the marvelous releasing power of Jesus Christ, nothing is impossible." Do that and live with verve and victory and enthusiasm, such as you have never had before. Leave those old negative defeats at the altar of God. And like Joan of Arc, let Him touch your bright and shining sword and storm the walls of defeat to conquer them.

Shoot for the moon. Even if you miss it, you will land among the stars. —Les Brown

CHAPTER 3

Begin With Love

A new commandment I give unto you, That ye love one another; as I have loved you, that ye also love one another.

—John 13:34

WITHOUT love, you are nothing; I am nothing; the world is nothing. If it were possible to sum up the teachings of Christianity in one word, that word would be *love*. "A new commandment I give unto you," said Jesus to His disciples at the Last Supper, "that ye love one another; as I have loved you, that ye also love one another," (John 13:34). And years later, the aged Apostle John gathered people around him and told them to love one another.

Some people mistake Christianity for a system of rules: "You shouldn't do this, you must do that." But what some interpret as rules are only what man has added. In its beginnings, in its essence, in the simple teachings of Jesus, Christianity is a religion of love. That is basic.

And this emphasis on love is not only for the purpose of making the earth a better world, although a better world will come when we truly love one another. The Gospel stresses love because a person will actually wither and die, ultimately, unless he has love in his heart, both for himself and other people. One of the greatest books on this subject was written by the late Smiley Blanton, with whom I had the honor to found The Blanton-Peale Institute of Religion and Health. Smiley Blanton was one of the great American psychiatrists of our day, one of the great teachers, one of the great lovers of humanity. He wrote a book entitled *Love Or Perish.* It's theme: Either you love or you will perish.

Here is one thought-provoking passage from the beginning of that book:

> To say that one will perish without love does not mean that everyone without adequate love dies. Many do, for without love the will to live is often impaired to such an extent that a person's resistance is critically lowered and death follows. But most of the time, lack of love makes people depressed, anxious, and without zest for life. They remain lonely and unhappy, without friends or work they care for, their life a barren treadmill, stripped of all creative action and joy.

Love or perish! No wonder Jesus makes love central to His whole teaching! If you are going to live creatively, you must learn to love.

A judge in Philadelphia, speaking of his experiences dealing with juveniles in trouble with the law, said that most of the young people who came before his court for discipline were hostile and aggressive. But their attitude didn't bother him nearly so much as the attitude of their parents. Often the child's father would be outraged: "Why do you do this to my boy?" he would ask. "Why bring him in here? Don't you know who I am?"

"But," said the judge, "never once did I see any of those fathers show any sign of affection for their teen-agers.

Never once did a father put his arm around his son or daughter. Never once did he even touch his child. When a parent will show love, even by a simple act of touching, there is an opportunity for redemption. Otherwise, young people die emotionally, they did mentally, they die in their personalities because of a lack of love."

Now, to avoid any misunderstandings when talking about love, you must first define it. The kind of love I am talking about is not the type that is dished up in television soap operas or in the movies. Neither is it the kind that revolves around romantic relationships. Of course, romantic love has its place in life, but it doesn't need any extra emphasis. It gets along pretty well on its own!

The kind of love I mean is a deep feeling for others, for people generally, that is hard to express. If you are seeking understanding and help from someone, you can experience this communication from a smile, a handshake, a pat on the shoulder, or a pat on the back. These gestures transmit a feeling that cannot easily be put into words. How do you express love? By sharing, by touching, by closeness to one another.

One of the most moving stories I ever heard came out of World War I. The story is about two brothers I knew. They hadn't seen each other for many months—from the time they left home to sail across the sea to Flanders. Then one night, some men coming out of the trenches passed a detachment of men going in to replace them. All of a sudden, in the light of the moon, these two brothers came face to face with each other, one going into the trenches, the other coming out.

Now, how would you think two soldiers, brothers, meeting each other for a moment under circumstances where the danger of death was constantly hanging over them—how would you think they would greet each other? They didn't say a word. They didn't ask, "How is Mom?" or "How is Dad?" or "How is Mary?" or "How is Genevieve?" or anything of the sort. They started punching each other, like they were boxing! The punches thudded from chest to chest. Then one brother said to the other, "See you, boy." The other said, "See you, kid." And they separated.

Men standing by understood. This was love in its deepest expression. Girls might embrace. Men often punch each other. But all who saw this expression of love were uplifted by it and trudged on up or down the trench, brushing tears from their eyes.

Love comes first in creative living . . . and to have it, you must love yourself. That is primary. That is the first thing that should be said: "Love yourself." Do you truly love yourself?

"Oh," you say, "that's easy. I sure do like myself. I am proud of myself."

But wait a minute. That isn't love. That is egotism. True love of yourself is having a deep, joyous respect for yourself, being mindful of your God-given abilities and capabilities and potentials and using them to the fullest extent possible.

The Gospel indicates that, without this wholesome loving respect for yourself, you cannot really love anyone else. It tells us, "Thou shalt love thy neighbor as thyself" (Matthew 19:19). This implies that if you don't love yourself, you won't love your neighbor. But if you do love and respect yourself as a child of God, then you can likewise love and respect another person as a child of God.

Every human being has a story. All you have to do is show people you like them, and presently they will start talking. I was asked one day, "Where do you get all your tales about people?" The answer is, from people. They are lovable, delightful. If you want people to like you, get up in the morning and say, "Lord, help me to love everyone I see today: help me at least to like them. Help me to see the good in them."

Some people seem to actually enjoy not liking people. It is the kind of enjoyment you derive from biting on an aching tooth: sadistic. Get to loving people and your whole personality will change, and love will come back to you.

I am giving you two simple rules for learning how to get people to like you: Develop an easy, relaxed attitude in your personal relationships. Then practice loving people.

I once had a friend whom I shall never forget. I first met him when I was a young minister. I was around 28 years old, slight, thin, not weighing more than 120 pounds. I had been invited to Syracuse to preach in a church where I was, without my knowing it, on trial as a candidate. It was a university church, with professors and students in the congregation. I sat almost lost in a big chair on the platform. Beside me was a huge man.

I leaned toward him. "Professor Tilroe," I asked, "I would be interested to know what subject you teach."

"I am Dean of the College of Public Speaking," he said.

I slid still lower in my chair.

Then he added, "I do not know anymore about it than you do. I just teach it." This comforted me a bit.

I gave my sermon, and evidently they couldn't find anyone else to take the church, for they called me. I was there for five years and, whenever I would get into any difficulty, I would see Professor Tilroe. He loved to go fishing. I always knew where to look for him: I would find him out along his favorite lake.

Once, when something bothered me, I joined him. We sat side-by-side fishing for some time, when he remarked plaintively, "Until you showed up, the fish were biting."

We had lunch, then fished some more without getting one single bite. Finally he asked, "What did you come to see me about?"

"I forget now," I said. And I *had* forgotten: All it took was snuggling up next to him. He was so great-hearted, he sent out love. His mere presence helped people.

So if you do not have a healthy spiritual self-esteem, by all means seek to have it. Pray about it; read the Bible; get closer to God. You will automatically learn to love yourself as you become increasingly aware of God's everlasting, unremitting, constant love for you.

One of the greatest statements ever made is this: "For God so loved the world, that He gave His only begotten Son, that whosoever believeth in Him should not perish, but have everlasting life" (John 3:16). If you were called upon to demonstrate love, what greater example could you give than this? It's the most poignant gift of love ever known in all the history of mankind. Its culmination was the crucifixion.

After scourging Jesus, putting a crown of thorns on His head, laughing Him to scorn, spitting on Him, showing Him every contempt, the Roman soldiers nailed Him to a cross. Then, raising the cross, they let it fall into the earth with a thud. It must have pulled every tendon and every muscle with excruciating pain. And Jesus, in body,

34

was human. Yet as He hung there, what did He say? "Father, forgive them; for they know not what they do" (Luke 23:34). What greater love could there be?

There is no circumstance in your life where God will not stand with you and help you, no matter what it is. He understands all your troubles, all your frustrations and disappointments. He understands your many weaknesses. He loves you.

A few years back, my wife and I rode with a taxi driver who was an interesting man. The name written on his license was Dutch, so I asked if he was from Europe.

"Yes," he said, "from Rotterdam."

"Well," I replied, "I was the minister of the old Dutch Reformed Church in New York City for fifty-two years."

"Oh," he commented in surprise. "Then you're Doctor Peale."

"Yes, sir," I said.

"I've been to your church," he continued, "but I didn't recognize you without your robe."

"Yes," I said, "there is a difference between a gown and a business suit." And we had a nice chat.

As we drove along, he asked, "Have you time to let me tell you a story? It is about the time I met God, and it shows how good God is. I have great faith, sir, and I know that I can never get outside the care and love of God.

"It was close to the end of World War II," he began. "I was a little boy. Our country had been ravaged. The conquerors had been driven out, but we were left absolutely destitute. We had ration stamps, but they weren't any good, for we had no food at all. There was no food in the warehouses or in the stores or in the country districts. Holland had been swept clean of foodstuffs.

"We were reduced to eating beets out of the fields. It was a kind of beet that is dangerous to eat without long cooking. Even then, if you don't accompany it with other food, the chemical reaction will bloat and distend the stomach. People have been known to die from the chemical that they absorbed from an overdose." He continued, "You know how beautiful Holland's tulips are? We dug the bulbs out of the ground and ate them. That was all we had. We were desperate.

"Then a notice from our pastor went around, telling us that there would be a meeting in the church. Since we were reduced to final circumstances, we would have a meeting and pray to God, telling Him we were His children and asking Him to feed us.

It was the only hope we had. The big church was packed; two thousand people were present. There was no sermon. We prayed for an hour or two. The pastor prayed. People prayed aloud all over the church. We sat there herded together, praying to God.

"I was only a little boy. But all of a sudden, I became aware that God was right there and I was almost frightened. I could feel Him in my heart. I knew that He was present, and I knew that He was going to take care of us poor starving people.

"Then we sang one of those old Dutch hymns of faith and we went out into the streets and back to our homes; and with a gnawing, empty stomach, I fell asleep.

"Early the next morning, we were awakened by the roar of a great armada of airplanes over Rotterdam, and there began a great shower of food. It seemed that the sky was full of great packages of food floating down to the streets of Rotterdam, filling the avenues with fine food.

And we ate. And we were saved."

The driver glanced back at us from the driver's seat, as he said, "As long as I live, I will believe that God heard those prayers and, out of His great heart of love, He fed his children."

And so do I believe it. And I am sure you do, also. He is a loving God. He loves you more dearly than your mother loves you, or your father, or your spouse. You are His child. So just get to know Him and trust His love. Then you will have that wholesome esteem for your own self that leads to having respect and love for all people.

The next thing, once you've learned to trust God in all things, is to make loving your neighbor a conscious daily practice. In a huge city, people come at you by the thousands. On the streets, there are so many that it bewilders you; and, when you are crowded into subways or fast-moving buses or trains with so many others, it often seems insufferable. But Jesus Christ said that we should love one another. So if you and I want to live creatively and grow spiritually, we must practice loving people, not as groups of people, but individually, in Jesus' name. And if each of us, loving himself as a child of God and loving Jesus, would really begin loving all people as our neighbors, why, we would change the world in no time.

Without love, we are nothing. The Bible tells us:

> I may have all knowledge and understand all secrets;
> I may have all the faith needed to move mountains—
> but if I have not love, I am nothing. I may give away
> everything I have, and even give up my body to be
> burned—but if I have not love, it does me no good.
> Love is patient and kind; love is not jealous, or con-

ceited, or proud; love is not ill-mannered, or selfish, or irritable; love does not keep a record of wrongs; love is not happy with evil, but is happy with the truth. Love never gives up: its faith, hope, and patience never fail. Love is eternal (1 Corinthians 13:2-8 GOOD NEWS FOR MODERN MAN—TODAY'S ENGLISH VERSION).

The most important thing a father can do for his children is to love their mother.

—The Rev. Theodore Hesburgh

CHAPTER 4

Discover Your Dreams

And [they] besought Him that they might only touch the hem of His garment; and as many as touched were made perfectly whole. —Matthew 14:36

EVERYONE has it in his heart, though perhaps he has never defined it, to be a well-integrated, organized, controlled, effective individual. This is a tall order and is often dependent upon resolving many complexities. But it just could be that we make the entire matter more complex than is necessary.

If a person is not satisfied with himself, there is a solution. First, of course, there has to be what sometimes has been called "divine discontent." Before we can ever become what we want to be, we must be dissatisfied with what we are. Having reached that first step on the ladder of self-improvement, we then come to the heart of the matter. The key to becoming what we want to be is found in the 14th chapter of Matthew, where there is a description of Jesus moving amid the multitude on the shores of the Sea of Galilee.

The people in those throngs were not well educated. But they seemed to possess that penetrating perception that God often gives to the humble and the simple. They recognized in Jesus of Nazareth an amazing power. They were conscious of it. It lured them. It fascinated them.

Instinctively, they knew that He had the answer to their lives. And they "Besought him that they might only touch the hem of His garment." Only the hem; that is the turned up part at the bottom. They figured that, if they could just get hold of the hem, something would happen to them. They weren't going to go to school to become skillful in the ways of faith. They were just going to get hold of the outward reaches of His garment. And the passage goes on to say, "and as many as touched were made perfectly whole." That is a powerful verse.

Don't be so complex about it all. Don't feel that you have to understand so much, or have to do so many things. It isn't so complicated. I don't want to oversimplify, but what this passage says is: If you want to be a better person, you should reach for Him and just get hold of something of His, even if it's only the hem of His garment. If your reaching is the real thing, if your desire is real, you will be made perfectly whole. Think of that. You'll no longer be defeated by your fears. You'll no longer be torn asunder by inner conflict. You'll no longer be defeated by evil in your nature. You'll no longer be divided. You will be made perfectly whole.

What, then, would you like to be? I suppose there has never been a child who has not asked his mother at some time: "Mother, what will I be when I grow up?" One of the most romantic dreams of childhood is "When I grow up, I'm going to be . . . ." It is this dream that lures us on and leads us to self-realization.

Did you ever want to be something? Do you still want to be? This is the motivation or the urge that Almighty God has put in all of us. We must strive until the story is ended. And man has unlimited scope of being.

Some time ago, I spoke at a large gathering at a machinery manufacturers' convention. There, I fell into conversation with a manufacturer who had the soul of a poet, even though, of necessity, he was a practical man, too. He told me he could imagine nothing more wonderful than "the astounding machines that American business is ordering from American science and that American science is delivering to American business." He pounded the table in his enthusiasm, as he said to me, "There is positively no limit to what a machine can do and be." He sounded like an evangelist when he said that; and I was impressed. He believed there were limitless possibilities in machinery. No wonder he was a leader in his field.

Every day, you read about some new technology that promises to revolutionize people's lives in some startling way. Today, there's hardly a business that isn't run by computers. No sooner does one computer come out into the marketplace, then a new one comes along to make the first one obsolete. The other day, I read an article about a young man, 39 years old, named Trip Hawkins, well known in the computer field as a genius. He's working on a machine that will enable the television viewer to interact with what he's watching on the TV screen and change the plot of the story. This may sound a little farfetched to believe, but who can say it will not happen?

I attended a banquet in Mansfield, Ohio, where I sat beside a man who is said by some to have been the greatest farmer who ever lived in the United States. Louis Bromfield was his name. He wrote a book called *Malabar Farm.* He also wrote a classic, entitled *My Ninety Acres.* In my estimation, it is one of the most beautiful books written in the past hundred years. He was a genius with words, but he was also a genius with soil. I said to him, "I understand, Mr. Bromfield, that you have done some great things with worn-out soil."

"There is no such thing as worn-out soil," Bromfield replied. "Man mistreats the soil. He draws from it its elements of fertility. But if you know how to restore those elements by means of scientific agriculture, there is positively no limit to what you can do with the soil." Here again was an enthusiast, and again I was impressed.

No limit to what you can do with a machine, no limit to what you can do with computers, no limit to what you can do with the soil, no limit to what can be done with non-human nature.

Well, if there is no limit to the possibilities in those realms, there is certainly no limit to what human beings, with God's help, can do with themselves! What is the highest form of God's creation? Human nature: with its weaknesses, but with its strength; with its defeat, but with its victory; with its sins, but with its goodness; with its illimitable possibility under God. What, then, would you like to be? You name it, and by God's grace you can be it.

You may say, "That is going too far. That is promising too much." But, mark you, I have not said you can attain this through your own strength, because you cannot. You are weak. You are of the world, earthy. But you are also of heaven, heavenly. And through God's grace, you can realize your highest dreams.

As a boy or girl, you had long, long thoughts of what you might be. Have you now become so old and tired and cynical that you have forgotten those dreams of your youth; those high expectations of yourself? Never lose them, no matter what. Lose your stock certificates, lose your property, but don't lose your dreams. For this urge to be some-one, to be something, was put into you by Almighty God. Hold it. And touch the hem of His garment.

Some months ago, in London, I stood outside Westminster Abbey looking at the statue of Abraham Lincoln just off Whitehall. Lincoln didn't quite make it into the inside of the Abbey. But he did get within a hun-dred yards of the front door. It is always an inspiration to wander through Westminster Abbey and study the effi-gies of great kings, queens, poets, and other personages. Then you can go outside and look up at the figure of Honest Abe. I stood there lost in admiration, thinking, *You sure have come a long, long way!*

He was born in the Kentucky wilderness, reared among the poor, drinking avidly of knowledge from a few books that he borrowed, without benefit of formal schooling, television, or even electric light. Just a lanky boy stretched out at night with a book in front of the open fire. How in the world did he ever get anywhere? Well, he had Weem's *Life of Washington,* he had Plato's *Republic,* he had the Holy Bible. And he had the ability to think and to pray and to dream. Moreover, he had a mother, one of the sweetest characters in history, Nancy Hanks.

As she did her housework, Nancy Hanks sang hymns, hymns about heaven. "There's a land that is fairer than day, And by faith we can see it afar . . ." But with scrub-bing and toiling, she worked her youth and strength away. And in her 30s, she was seized with the milk sickness, a terrible scourge that swept across those frontier commu-nities, and she succumbed.

Later, a wonderful stepmother came into the family. She often called her tall, ungainly, lanky son to her side and, with all her aversion to sin and crudity and poverty and lack of culture, she said to him: "Abe, be somebody." Years later, when at the Capitol in Washington he took the oath of office as President, I wonder if he did not hear out of the yesterdays the soft, sweet, yet strong voice of a pioneer mother saying, "Abe, be somebody."

Now, I realize there are many people who would say this aspiration is corny. But if we Americans have come to the point where we think it's corny to want to be someone, then we are corny ourselves, and we have no relatedness to the great past or the potential future.

Be someone! And what is that supposed to mean? Nowadays, the idea is to become a V.I.P.—very important person. Well, I have a lot of respect for some V.I.P.'s. But some of those whose publicity agents get them a big play leave me cold.

Or the idea is to be a big shot. What is a big shot? I've heard a big shot defined as a little shot who keeps on shooting. But there are many phonies among big shots, as well as a great many fine people.

In any case, to be a V.I.P., a big shot, or a celebrity is not a goal worthy of the desire of a real person. I would say a real person wants to be his best self. That is, he wants to realize all the potential that he has. He wants to step up into focus every God-given ability with which he is endowed. He wants to use himself to the best advantage, not for himself, but for the world and for God. To be someone in that true sense is the highest realization of yourself as a child of God. And a mother tries to instill in her children this longing for achievement.

We need a reassessment of values. The aim of life is to be an organized, integrated, dedicated, useful, outgoing, loving, and helpful individual worthy of the approval of God. So touch the hem of His garment right now and become completely whole.

One evening in May, I gave a speech in Jamestown, N.Y. It was lilac time in Western New York State: blue sky, green hills, the fragrance of lilacs. The stern red-brick buildings of the cities of that part of the Empire State have a strength about them that appeals to me as an old up-stater. On this occasion, I spoke to a gathering of more than one thousand people in the ballroom of the Hotel Jamestown. When I arrived at the hotel, the elevators were jammed with people going up to the ballroom, and the entire place was a picture of confusion.

Running one of the elevators was a girl—happy, genial, unperturbed—who said to me, "Get in here. I'll give you an express to the ballroom. We'll bypass this crowd." And on the way up, she said, "I know you're the speaker. You've got to get up there to do some thinking about your speech, don't you?"

"How right you are!" I replied, and added, "You know, I like you."

"Do you, now?" said she.

"I really do," I told her. "The Lord has given you a tremendous personality. You're happy, things don't irritate you, you exude friendliness and goodness. I like you. You're a nice girl."

"Girl?" she queried.

"Yes," I said, "girl."

"It'll surprise you to know I have two sons in college," she informed me. "How's that for being a girl?"

"You're still a girl," I insisted. "You're a girl till you die. So you've got two sons in college?"

"Yes, and I'm putting them through myself. I got a scholarship for one, got a little help that way. But I'm putting my two boys through college."

I asked where her husband was. She merely said he had gone and did not elaborate. A mother running an elevator. She told me she also had another job. "I would like the privilege of shaking your hand," I said. "You are a great woman." I added, "I hope your boys will be rich and famous."

In retrospect, that was a stupid thing for me to say. Why I ever said it, I wouldn't know—just trying to be nice, I guess.

She quite rightly answered, "I don't care if they get rich or famous. I just hope that they'll never let me down, that they'll be good, clean, decent boys all their lives."

"With a mother like you, how can they help it?" I said. "God bless you."

"God is the One who will do it," she answered.

Not long ago, I revisited Bellefontaine, Ohio. Some of the uninitiated pronounce it *bell fon tane*. But it's not a sophisticated place. It's just plain old *bell fountain*. And that's where I went to school as a boy. We lived at 308 North Detroit Street, in a plain house with one bathroom and no picture windows. Just a square house with a room on this side, a room on that side, a hall in the middle, and three or four rooms upstairs. There was a coal furnace down below, too. That was it. It was the parsonage occupied by my father, the Rev. Charles Clifford Peale. (Nowadays, the church has a fine modern parsonage, but it didn't have it in my time.)

The last time I was in Bellefontaine, I walked up North Detroit Street and stopped in front of number 308, remembering the past. In those days, across the street had been a little candy store. When you opened the door, a bell would ring way back in the cool recesses. The store was run by an old lady, and the candy was the sweetest I ever ate. I can't buy it anymore, because the store is gone—and that is just as well, for it wouldn't taste the same. Candy tastes sweeter to a boy of eight or ten than it does to a fellow who is much older.

But as I stood there gazing at the old house, it was as though I could see the door open and my mother come out. My mother had fair skin and blue eyes and blond hair. Although it was an ancient style, I always seem to picture her in a dress with one of those chokers at the neck that came way up under the chin and held a women's head up straight. And she would have her hair piled up some way—and perched on top of it was a big hat. And those big balloon sleeves—I could see my mother coming out of the house like that and down the steps. I remembered sitting on that porch with her years ago, when she had been telling me that we had to economize, that we couldn't have this or that, because we didn't have the money. She said, "I won't go in debt." That sounds old-fashioned, nowadays, doesn't it? She said, "No one should ever go in debt. Don't get it until you can pay for it."

But it annoyed me, so I said, "Mother, I want to be someone. I want to amount to something. I'm going to go out and make money and I'm going to come back to this town with enough money to buy and sell some of these people around here."

"Well, now, Norman," she remonstrated, "I didn't raise you for that. I don't care about your having money. I want you to have enough money to pay your bills, but I don't want you to make money the aim of your life."

"Well, all right," I declared, "then I'll be Governor of Ohio, instead."

But my mother talked me out of that. "Ambition, Norman," she said, "is good, if God controls it. There are dedicated men with money, who use their money for God, and there are dedicated men who become governors. But what I want you to be is a clean, decent, honorable, upright Christian man with love in your heart, serving God and His children. And I want you so to live that when you finish your course of life, long after I have preceded you, I'll meet you somewhere in the eternities of our Lord."

That sounds sentimental. But maybe we *should be* sentimental. This is the ideal that Christian mothers have put into us—or rather that they have fanned into flame, because it was God Himself who planted in us the instinct to be children of God. So touch the hem of His garment, that you may be made perfectly whole.

*To know one's self is the true;
to strive with one's self is the
good; to conquer one's self is
the beautiful.*   —Joseph Roux

CHAPTER 5

Ask God for Great Things

Jesus said unto him, If thou canst believe, all things are possible to him that believeth.

—*Mark 9:23*

ONE of the outstanding characteristics of this age is the widespread use of prayer. People are putting far more emphasis on prayer today than they did formerly. The people who say that religion is on the decline are not fully aware of what actually goes on in this country. Elders throughout history have fretted that the younger generation has lost the sense of its heritage and religious values.

But a recent Gallup Youth Survey demonstrates that a majority of the young people of America continues to consider religion important in their lives. And another recent poll conducted by the *Reader's Digest* concludes that 75 percent of those interviewed approve of prayer in public schools. Again and again, I am moved and inspired by the evidences that prayer and faith are practiced.

For example, Mrs. Peale and I were in a television studio where a filmed program of ours was to be shown, so the station invited us to appear "live," as people call it. We were ushered into the manager's office. Mrs. Peale had walked in ahead of me when, to my surprise, the secretary, who gave me the impression from her manner and dress of being a sophisticated woman, said to me, "Would you mind waiting a moment, Doctor Peale?"

She shut the door and stood there, lips trembling, tears in her eyes. "I haven't been religious," she said. "But I have been up against a crisis in my life. I watched you preaching on television. You seemed to believe that prayer is something everyone can use, so I began to pray." And her face brightened as she added, "I can't begin to tell you how praying has changed everything for me."

Let me give you another illustration. I had made an appointment with a barber. (It is a strange day, isn't it, when you have to make an appointment for a barber. In my youth, you went to the barber shop, read old magazines, and waited.) This time, I went at the appointed time, and got into the chair. I noticed that the woman in charge of the shop was quite agitated. She was pacing the floor, talking about a coronary attack. And I came to understand that it was her husband, the owner of the shop, who had had the attack. Several men in the shop were trying to explain to her about a coronary when my barber, not knowing me except that I was called "Doctor," said to them, "Here is a doctor now in my chair; let him tell her."

"I am not that kind of doctor," I said, "but I have been involved in a good many such cases." And I asked how long it was since her husband had the attack. Told that it had been three days ago, I said, "I think you can feel that the crisis is past and he will come through all right."

As I was standing at the cash register paying my bill, I tried to talk to her without the others hearing. "Do you have a good doctor?"

"Yes, indeed," she said.

"Why don't you also put your husband in the hands of

another doctor, too? I mean the Great Physician. Just pray about this situation and put your husband in the hands of God. Believe that the Great Physician will heal him."

Then I became aware of a stillness in that barber shop, and a rather rough-looking boy spoke up and said, "Yes, Mary. Everybody in this whole town is praying for Jim. I'm praying for him. He is going to be all right. You just pray for him, too."

I turned to look at those men gathered around me. And I knew that Jesus Christ was in that barber shop, that He had laid His healing touch on everyone there.

Years ago, people would have been embarrassed by a conversation like that. Now it is a common, everyday procedure. Everywhere, people have learned, and are learning, that they can solve their problems by prayer.

How do you go about praying in such a way that you will get a solution to your problem? First, I think we should pray to God to tell us what to do and how to do it. A human being is prone to error, full of the possibilities of mistakes. A young man asked me the other day, "Why do I do so many stupid things?" I couldn't help him because, as I told him, I was still trying to find the answer to that question for myself. But I have discovered that when I really pray, I get a sense of rightness, of security that I do not otherwise possess.

Not long ago, the leaders of this country made a prayerful decision to deploy U.S. troops to the Persian Gulf. All across this great country, prayers followed our courageous young men and women as they took their places in the desert, ready to do their part to preserve freedom.

There were few streets in America that were not adorned with yellow ribbons, this country's sign of faith and support for the great sacrifice our troops were being asked to make. Each ribbon represented one (or many) prayers being said. It also represented the hope that, one day, differences would be settled by negotiation and not on battlefields. I cannot remember a time, when as a whole nation, we so earnestly looked to God for direction and guidance, when so many publicly prayed, acknowledging that God is our ultimate source of hope.

The *Reader's Digest* once printed an article entitled "The Case of The Railway Man's Arm." This story intrigued me. The man's arm had been horribly mutilated, caught between two freight cars. The physician said, "Immediate amputation is the only answer," and the patient was prepared for the operation.

But then the doctor just happened to look at the patient's face, which was saying mutely, "I'd rather die than lose that arm."

The doctor thought, *You will die; I can't save that arm.* Then he asked himself if he wasn't doing the easier thing, instead of trying the more difficult and revolutionary operation. While his assistants waited, he astonished them by saying, "I am going to try to save that arm."

After 3½ hours, during which the man's blood pressure dropped and his heart almost stopped, the operation was concluded. For ten days, the patient hovered between life and death, and the physician berated himself for not amputating. But at the end of 45 days, when he took off the cast with all the hospital personnel gathered around to watch, there was a beautiful arm, healing perfectly.

Later the man said, "Doctor, thank you for saving my arm. I really do appreciate it."

"I shouldn't have performed that operation," said the

doctor to his grateful patient.

"But I knew you would do it," the man replied.

"How did you know?" asked the doctor.

"I couldn't speak; I was in a daze. But I prayed to God, asking Him to tell you to save my arm, and to tell you how to do it. And God told me you would save it."

"That explains the conflict in my mind," said the surgeon. "And the feeling of certainty that I could save your arm, the conviction that I could do it."

That operation was a great demonstration of surgical skill and the power of prayer. If you pray to God and believe, He will tell you what to do and how to do it. (See Mark 9:23).

I realize that in all such illustrations, there is an area of dispute. But I long ago got over the idea of giving both the negative and positive sides. There are plenty of people to provide the negative. I provide the positive. I am merely giving documentary demonstrations of prayer's activity in daily life.

There is a second thing I would say about prayer, and that is the importance of asking God for what you want. Have the courage to ask Him for great things. If you don't ask for great things, you won't get them. But you must be willing to take "no" for an answer. Sometimes you are benefited by having a "no" said to your prayers.

When she was only 12 years old, I asked our daughter Elizabeth how she prayed. Her method was simple, but impressive. Most of us make prayers so terribly complicated. That is why Jesus said, "Come as a little child" (see Luke 18:16-17). Elizabeth said, "There is nothing to it. I just ask the Lord to help me."

And that is all there is to it. Just become childlike

enough, simple enough to believe that, if you ask Him to help you, He will. And be ready to accept a "no" answer, if it comes. I had the hardest time getting over the need for scientific methods, the need to demonstrate how prayer works. But I wasn't going to have any part of scientifically explaining it. I prided myself on having a cold, rational mind. But over and over, I continued to see evidence of God answering simple pleas for help. That was it: The power of answered prayer has always convinced me that God hears us, and He answers: sometimes with a "no," sometimes with a "yes," sometimes with a "wait a while."

There are so many people who want to argue about everything. Those are the people who show no evidence of faith in anything. For example: I was sitting in a hotel one night, and the hotel manager was telling me about his brother-in-law, a vice admiral in the United States Navy. Some months before, he had been in command of an aircraft carrier in the Mediterranean. One day, they sent out 40 boys in planes on maneuvers, and while they were out, a heavy fog came up. The planes circled the ship, but they couldn't land and were running out of fuel.

"This admiral brother-in-law of mine is not what you would call a praying man," said the hotel keeper, "but he thought about those boys, about their mothers, their fathers, and their wives, and didn't know what to do. Going to his cabin, he gathered together his officers and said 'Gentlemen, we come of praying people. We must pray.'

"Of course there was a scientist present. 'How can you get rid of fog by prayer?' he asked. 'Fog is a natural phenomenon.'

" 'The movements of the earth are God's,' said the admiral. And he asked the Lord to bring in his 40 boys.

"The fog parted, those boys got down on deck, and the fog closed in again."

Do you have any trouble with that story? Are you asking, "What about the times when the fog doesn't part?" Well, we aren't talking about the times when it doesn't; we are talking about the time when it did. And if it will do that once, there must be spiritual laws that we have not yet mastered, that we have never fully observed. When we master them, then there will be tremendous power ready for our use.

There is a third aspect of prayer we need to consider. We pray, not to get, but to have fellowship with God. We pray to bring meaning into our lives. So we ought to pray that God be in us and that we may be in God. I, personally, believe that you won't be healthy, really healthy, unless you are in God and God is in you.

Since the wall in Berlin came down, there has been a resurgence of talk about the divisions of Germany that followed World War II and the Holocaust. Those days were certainly dark times in Europe, leaving millions dead and millions more shattered by devastating losses. Dr. Viktor Frankl, himself a survivor, describes his psychiatric theory, known as "Logo Therapy," in his book *Man's Search for Meaning*. Logo Therapy means the medical healing of men's souls. He spoke of Sigmund Freud, whose emphasis was on sex, and of Alfred Adler, whose emphasis was on power. Dr. Frankl claims that the principle human drive is the drive for God.

Today, as well as then, too many people suffer from profound neuroses because they do not have spiritual meaning in their lives. Furthermore, Frankl states, it is no longer unsophisticated to seek after spiritual understanding; the real pathology of our time is that thousands of people have no depth of spiritual meaning.

These ideas promoting the relationship between psychiatry and Christianity have risen not only in Europe, but in America, as well. Some time ago, Dr. Smiley Blanton and I started a counseling service to show that psychiatric medicine and religion are teammates. He and I worked tirelessly to show people how to get an inner sense of spiritual meaning into their lives through prayer and faith. Today, The Blanton-Peale Institute of Religion and Health in New York City is a living testament to the curative force of the two therapies. This work, and the work of Dr. Frankl, have brought to this century the understanding that a person has to be spiritually alive to be physically alive.

Finally, one of the best ways to pray is to ask for nothing except God Himself. A young man once told me how he had struggled and been defeated, how many conflicts he had endured, how he prayed to no avail. "But one night," he said, "it was about two o'clock in the morning and I couldn't sleep. I got up and paced the floor. I didn't know what else to do. I even thought of throwing myself out the window. Finally, I knelt down by the bed and prayed, saying, 'God, I don't ask You for a thing. I just ask You for Yourself. Take me, and give me Yourself.'"

Then, instantly, he had a sense of peace and quietness. He became sleepy, fell into bed, and slept the rest of the night and on into the morning. "I awakened a new man; every circumstance started to change for me," he said. "When I found God, I found a new life."

The trouble, perhaps, is that we pray too much for things. Just pray for God, until He floods your being with

Himself. It will bring everything into its proper place. There isn't a human being alive whose life cannot be completely changed by this process. You have to be spiritually alive to be physically alive. Just pray that you may have God, and that God may have you.

Our prayers are not answered when we are given what we ask, but when we are challenged to be what we can be.

—Morris Adler

CHAPTER 6

Get Excited

Whom having not seen, ye love; in whom, though now ye see Him not, yet believing, ye rejoice with joy unspeakable and full of glory. —1 Peter 1:8

A MERICAN author Eric Hoffer has said, "When people are bored, it is primarily with their own selves that they are bored."

Are *you* bored? Suppose you answer this question privately in your own mind. Are you irked part of the time or all of the time? Or, on the contrary, are you excited much of the time or all of the time? Do you find that life is dull, or is it mostly fascinating?

It is surprising how often I have read that the American people are bored. I don't understand it, for there is more opportunity in this country for the average man and woman than anyplace in the world. I say this with conviction, for I have traveled the world over. And there are many countries I like very much. But I have never found any country anywhere that is superior to the United States of America. There are more goods, more services, more values here than any other place I have been.

Of course, there are some people who seem to be bored either because they are fed-up with themselves, or because it reflects a trend they want to affect. If you act bored, then you're supposed to be "in." But the whole thing seems rather stupid, because how can you be happy and excited about life, if you act bored?

In his book, *Human Problems and How To Solve Them,* Dr. Charles Curtis put together some of the most common statements he hears people say every day. Here are some of them: "Life's a drag." "I'm fed up." "That tics me off." "That bugs me." "Everything's a mess." "I'm pooped." "I'm bored stiff."

Well, I've heard people of every age say those things. But there are also others, the really "in" people, the *real* sophisticates, who talk differently. Their actual statements are these: "Life is terrific, and I mean terrific!" "Everything's great, really great!" "I feel sensational." "What a thrill!" "What do you know! Another fantastic day!" "This is really living!" "This is it and I don't mean maybe." "Bored? Are you kidding? Life is fabulous!" Untold millions have found the secret—the secret of how to change boredom into excitement.

What secret have they discovered? Well, it is described in the Bible. Now many people write off the Bible as a dull book, which proves conclusively that they have never *really* read it. And they write off Christianity as a dull religion, which proves conclusively that they have never *really* been exposed to it. There are some people who, when they talk about Christianity, get pained expressions on their faces, as if they were related to an undertaker! Well, if those people would only read this: In 1 Peter 1:8, it says: "Rejoice with joy unspeakable and full of glory."

What a sentence! *Unspeakable!* That is to say, you cannot describe it in words. It is a joy and an excitement that is absolutely devoid of the power to define it; so great, you cannot fully explain it. That is not any old dull Christianity! *Full of glory!* That means bigger than big; that means huger than huge; something full of glory towers over everything!

This little, narrow-minded idea some people get of Christianity as just some dull, nice philosophical-theological doctrine is a crime against humanity! This faith that Jesus Christ set loose in the world is an absolute guarantee that, if you accept it, you will never be bored from that day until the day you die. You will be excited, fantastically, fabulously so, all the days of your life. What we need is a rebirth of the ability to describe Christianity as it really is, a great, joyful faith that transforms the world.

How can the American people be written off as bored when millions of them, through a new spiritual experience, have found excitement?

Now, how can *you* get this kind of attitude? The best way is to wake up and come alive.

There are many people who go through life asleep! The dictionary definition says that a bored person is one who is wearied by dullness. He is uninteresting company because he is comatose. He is the victim of tedium and ennui. (Pretty good words!) You might say that the bored person is a person who is asleep; his senses are not reacting, there is no profound relationship between him and life. He is discontented; he lacks interest in anything.

One night, as I went back to the motel after delivering a speech in an Indiana town, I convinced myself that I had really worked hard on that speech and deserved something to eat. Noticing a diner on the corner, I figured it must be a good place because there were trucks parked all around it. Truck drivers know a good eating place! If you are looking for a place along the road, see where they stop.

It may not be fancy, but the food certainly will be good. So I went in. Several truck drivers were sitting up at the counter putting away a big meal. And the man behind the counter looked like he was an ex-truck driver! He had great big arms, his shirtsleeves were rolled up, and he wore a white chef's hat on his head. He plunked his big hands down on the counter and asked me, "What do you want, brother?"

"Make it a double hamburger and a cup of coffee," I replied. As I waited for my order, I happened to notice two signs above a display that held boxes that looked like aspirin boxes. One sign said, "No-Nod Tablets" and the other said, "No-Sleep Tablets." I asked the big man behind the counter, "What are those tablets?"

"Well," he answered, "these truck drivers have long-night hauls and they must keep awake. So they come in here and have some coffee and a hamburger, and I often sell them one of those boxes. The no-sleep tablet is equivalent to about five cups of coffee. You take one of those tablets and you won't sleep. The no-nod tablet is equivalent to about two cups of black coffee. You take that and you won't nod."

"Brother, you've given me an idea," I said. "Where do you get those tablets in quantity?"

"What do you want to know for?" he asked.

"I happen to be a minister and a speaker, and I'd like to buy about three thousand boxes of those pills and pass them out to my audiences!"

Ignoring my attempt at humor, he plunked his hands down on the counter again and said, "That isn't what they need. You just give them a good, lively Gospel sermon and that'll wake 'em up! Anyone who goes to church with a sleepy attitude toward life and toward the world has missed the entire meaning of life!"

I have rarely felt more alive than I did the evening a full-harvest moon rose over the mountain at my farm in Dutchess County. The mist was in the valley, the shadows fell among the trees; the air was crystal-clear. My wife and I stood under the trees and worshiped Almighty God. It was really exciting!

"But," you may ask, "what can remind me of God, if I'm walking on a crowded city street? I can hardly see the moon from there!" Well, exercise your imagination. Think of the surge and the throb of any city; the conflict, the struggle, the rising, the falling, the grappling of an enormous city. It is filled with power, and God is there working out the greater day that is to be. And that should wake you up, make you alive to the possibilities of life.

The bored person has no sense of challenge; he does not give of himself to some great cause. He is just a dull, inert sleepyhead. He sees nothing in the world that beckons him. But the person who is excited about life never stops trying. No matter what the circumstances, he is in there fighting, and that is why his life continues to be filled with excitement.

While traveling in East Africa a few years ago, I received a phone call from a man who said, "I have just heard that you are in town and I've simply got to see you."

I explained that I was on my way to the airport.

"That doesn't make any difference," he persisted. "I will come to your hotel and take you to the airport."

"Thank you, but I already have someone to take me to the airport," I told him.

"Dismiss him; I'm taking you to the airport!"

I got the determination of his spirit and decided to meet this gentleman.

On the way to the airport, he told us how something I had written had pulled him through a deep, dark discouragement in his life. Here is his story: He was an accountant for the government of Kenya while the British were still there as a colonial power. He prosecuted cases for the government, preparing the accountant's case against delinquent individuals. And there was one big businessman in Kenya who was prosecuted heavily. This government official assisted in the case.

Then certain changes were made, and he lost his job. He tried to start his own business, but was having a poor go at it. He felt all along that there was something working against him, but he did not know what. Anyway, he read these words I wrote: pray, think, believe, and fight. Those four words, he said, sustained him in his discouragement. And one day, while he was praying, it came to him to see the businessman in whose prosecution he had assisted. He actually asked the man if he could do some work for him.

The man shook his head in disbelief. "Do you think that I would hire you, after what you did to me?"

"But," my friend said, "everything I did to you was honest. You were dishonest, and we had to prosecute you and get a judgment against you. I was doing my job and I would do it all over again, because, at that time, you certainly weren't straight!"

The man sat silently, considering what my friend had said. Finally he spoke. "I do need a new accounting firm, and I'm going to take you on. The reason I'm going to take you on is that I know that you are incorruptible."

"And," said my friend to his new employer, "don't ever try to corrupt me!"

"I wouldn't try, because I know it's absolutely impossible!" said the businessman. "If you will take my accounts, I will be glad to be your client."

"I'll take them, as long as they are straight and honest. But if they are not, I will make them public," declared the accountant.

The businessman sat back in awe and said, "I didn't know anyone like you existed anymore. You have the job!" And he extended his hand to my friend.

This man has built a huge, successful accounting firm. "Life is great," he told me, "as long as you stay in there fighting." Be alive to the possibilities of life. Wake up!

Several years ago, I went to South Jersey on the Erie-Lackawanna Railroad to give a speech. A man walked into the car and sat down next to me. He was a congenial kind of a character and asked me where I was going.

"I'm going to a big laundry convention tonight," I told him enthusiastically.

"I'm going there, too!" he exclaimed. "As a matter of fact, I am the principal speaker."

"That's odd," I said. "I thought I was the principal speaker!" As we talked on, it seems that he was the principal humorist who was to speak ahead of me, and I was to give the principal speech. Anyway, there on the train, he showed me some posters with his picture. They said, "The greatest humorist in the United States. The funniest man alive."

"Is that the way you advertise yourself?" I asked.

"Yes," he said, "I always connect."

"That's great," I gulped, wishing secretly that he would

be on *after* my speech was delivered!

Anyway, we arrived at the convention and the chairman introduced the humorist: "Ladies and Gentlemen," he said, "you're going to have the best laughing experience of your life! Hang on to your seats, because you are going to be hysterical with laughter." Well, he overbuilt him! My friend got up and threw out his first joke. It got kind of a polite response, which I thought was strange, for it was a real powerful joke. Then he put out another one and got a few titters. And the third one only evoked a few sickly smiles, except for me—I was laughing my head off! Every once in a while, he would lean down to me and say, "It sure is a tough crowd!" When he sat down, he was perspiring and looked discouraged.

Then came my turn. I had a couple of jokes, but was afraid to use them. But would you believe it? They laughed in my serious places! I leaned down to my friend, completely perplexed. "You're right, it sure is a tough crowd!"

It was one of the most disastrous speaking experiences I have ever had in my whole life! On the way home, Bill said, "Norman," (by this time we were calling each Norman and Bill) "have you got a speaking engagement tomorrow night? If not, go out and get yourself one. Don't take a licking for more than twenty-four hours!"

"Yes, I do have one," I told him.

"Fortunately, I have one, too," he said. When we left each other at the ferry boat, he grabbed me by the hand and said, "We won't take a licking, will we, old boy? Let's go right back at them and fight it through."

His psychology was excellent. Everyone in this world is going to experience defeat of some kind, sometime, somewhere. That is the way life is made; but life can be so exciting if you keep going. Oliver Wendell Holmes once said, "To reach the port of heaven, we must sail sometimes with the wind and sometimes against—but we must sail, not drift or lie at anchor."

Keep your thoughts conditioned to excitement. Never think of life as a bore. Make it alive, by thinking alive. Anyone can change his thoughts, if he uses discipline. There is not enough emphasis on the disciplinary control of thoughts these days, for you can, as Plato said, do anything with your thoughts if you take charge of them. If you are thinking dull, gloomy, discouraging thoughts, substitute bright, happy, optimistic, positive thoughts.

For many years, the Rev. Eugene McKinley Pierce was my associate at Marble Collegiate Church. When he went into the hospital for surgery, I went to see him. "Mac," as we called him, was in bed opening mail. He was having a good day when I saw him. The day before had been a dark, hard day. Mrs. Pierce and I talked about it. "Was Mac discouraged yesterday?" I asked. "He seems fine now!"

Mrs. Pierce pointed to her necklace. "See these pearls? Mac gave them to me for Christmas. They aren't the greatest pearls in the world. But I love them and wear them quite often. As I was sitting by his bed and casually touching them, a thought came to mind. 'Mac,' I said, 'let's start thinking of every wonderful experience we've had in our lives, one for each of these pearls.'"

Mrs. Pierce continued: "We started away back when we were first in love and that was the first pearl. Then we went along to our wedding day and then to our first baby. And our first church to serve, and so on, all the way down the string of pearls. When we finished with the last pearl," she said, "all the dark shadows had gone and happiness reigned in our minds and in our hearts."

You, too, can shift from gloominess to happiness, from dullness to vibrancy, from boredom to excitement. Wake up, change your thinking, and see how good life can be!

The tragedy of life is not that it ends so soon, but that we wait so long to begin it.

—Richard L. Evans

CHAPTER 7

Seek His Presence

His disciples came to Him and awoke Him, saying, Lord, save us, we perish. And He saith unto them, Why are ye fearful, O ye of little faith? Then He arose, and rebuked the winds and the sea; and there was a great calm.

—Matthew 8:25-26

BEFORE making an address in a Midwestern town one evening, I, with a dozen other men, was entertained at dinner. The discussion, as you might imagine, covered politics, international affairs, domestic problems, and finally got around to religion. The way that subject was reached is interesting. A young doctor in the group had been giving his views in a way that led me to believe he was a solid thinker. So I asked him about the best way to deal with people who become emotional and nervous under pressure. I asked him if he thought that I, as a pastor, could render any contribution.

"You can render a more important contribution than I," he answered quickly. "If people want to live peacefully with their nerves, all they need to do is to practice their religion." The physician continued: "I had drifted away from the church, never read the Bible, never prayed. I had become almost an unbeliever. But when I got out of the army and resumed my private practice, I began to notice a great change among people. Formerly, I had been able to cure some of them with medicine. Now, I have discovered that medicine alone cannot do the job. They are not living right; they are not thinking right; they are not trusting God as they should."

Later, I received a letter from a physician in an upstate New York town. I do not know this man, but I like him. He said he had just finished reading *The Power of Positive Thinking* and that he was recommending the book to several patients whose nerves were making their bodies ill. To quote him:

> I live in a small town made up of Protestants, Catholics, and Jews. About 60 percent of my patients are spiritually ill. You might even call them neurotic. It is almost useless to refer patients—as we desperately need to do—to a priest, a minister, or a rabbi because, in our section of the country, spiritual advisers have not come to realize that modern souls are sick to such an extent that their organs are in pain. I hope, in time, they will understand the relationship between sick souls and sick bodies.

Nowadays, scientifically trained, thoughtful medical men are telling people what preachers have been telling them for years: To live a normal, happy, healthy, effective life, you must live in company with, and under the direction of, Jesus Christ. I am no physician, although at one time I thought I would be, but I have a great love, respect, and veneration for the practitioners of medicine.

They will tell you that an agitated state can produce all kinds of disease symptoms. One doctor reports that a man came to him complaining of a "terrible stomach condition"; that he could not eat a square meal, and always had to take medication to stop the pain he suffered after a meal. The doctor gave him a thorough examination and found nothing physically wrong. He then inquired about his habits, and found that his patient was a speculator in the stock market. He waited with bated breath for the financial news to come off the press, then he took it to the table with him so that he could analyze it.

Naturally, after dinner, he had to take something to settle his stomach. When this man sold all the highly speculative stocks, and retained only sound investments, he could eat whatever he wanted without distress. "His only trouble was stress and nerves," the doctor concluded.

Another doctor tells of a man who lost 22 pounds he could not afford to lose. He was so tense and nervous that his friends were worried about him. He had been married for 20 years; one day, his wife—who was a vigorous, healthy woman—suddenly died. His friends expected him to go to an early grave. But to their surprise, he began to gain weight and soon was back in excellent health.

An investigation revealed that this man had been raised by a domineering mother. When he married, he did not really marry a wife, but a woman who was the replica of his mother. This girl was sweetness and light throughout the honeymoon, but it was a short honeymoon. Soon she demanded that he bring home his entire paycheck to her. She doled out his spending money, made him budget his expenses, and dominated him for 20 years. He became nervous and highstrung, lost weight, became a sick man. Why? What was eating at him? Something that he never would have admitted, which instinctively he would have repudiated as unworthy: He unconsciously resented his wife. Her death relieved him, and soon his health was restored.

For years, many researchers believed that there was a mind-body connection where the nervous system altered the immune system. Recently, doctors from Massachusetts General Hospital and the University of Pennsylvania discovered what many of us have known for a long time, that stress makes many diseases worse. The doctors found the first evidence of an anatomical connection between the nervous system and the immune system. "There is no question," says Dr. Brian Nickoloff, a physician at the University of Michigan, "that some diseases, even common ones, are made worse by stress: financial losses, a death in the family."

We say sometimes that our nerves are in bad shape, in the slang phrase, "shot to pieces." Now, the chances are there is nothing wrong with the actual nerves, those messengers that run like telephone wires from the brain down to the ends of the fingers. Where then is the trouble? The trouble is in the mind—in the switchboard. The nerve endings are getting all kinds of conflicting, counteracting, canceling messages and don't know what to do. The trouble is with the operator who runs the switchboard; in this case, the mind.

There was a telephone strike in New York some years ago, and officials of the telephone company had to operate the long-distance network manually. One of the telephone men took me into a vast room, where inexperienced men were working the system in the vain hope that they were making the right connections. If a customer called Los Angeles, he was likely to get Boston. There was confusion everywhere. Now, you would not think for one minute of trying to operate that kind of switchboard, would you? But you *are* operating a far more complicated "switchboard" all the time in the conduct of your nervous system. And your very life and happiness depend on *your* operation of this switchboard. You cannot do this without expert guidance; you cannot do it successfully, unless the Great Master who made the switchboard, and who understands it, tells you how to operate it. The minute that happens, you will know how to relax and live peacefully with your nerves.

Your physiological nerves are probably all right. A thousand-to-one odds say they are healthy; but it is the *control* of your nerves that is important. How, then, do you control them? Here are some simple exercises. Practice them until they become second nature to you. Practice the healing, disciplining, controlling presence of Jesus Christ. Get beyond the idea that He is a mystical, theoretical teacher who lived nearly 2000 years ago. *Believe,* until you have no doubt about it, that He is by your side helping you constantly. (See Matthew 8:25-26.)

Another doctor I know occasionally preaches to me about slowing down—and properly so. Then I preach to him about slowing down—he is always on the go, helping people. Although he drives himself at a terrific pace, he is a shining example of a controlled, disciplined, well-organized, properly functioning, impressive personality. He is an unusually inspiring person.

One day in his office, I asked him: "How do you keep control of your nerves?" He looked across the desk at me and said, "The Lord is here with me. I put my trust in Him. When I am going at a high pace, and begin to feel tense, I stop";—and these are his exact words—"I stop and say, 'Look Lord, I am running a little fast, not quite on the beam. Lord, let me feel Your touch.' Then I lean against the desk for just a minute and say, 'Let me feel Your quieting presence.' Then He touches me and I am quite all right again, and there is a great calm." So said the doctor, with sincerity.

You may ask, "Can the Lord actually be with you?" I believe He is. Sometime we are going to discover the remarkable resources of the human mind.

At Duke University, another group of research scientists made experiments that show that the human mind can pass barriers of time and space. And a man once wrote me, about some advice I had given on how to cultivate a peaceful attitude. I had suggested visualizing some beloved and peaceful scene. "Take your mind back into it and live it again," I had written. "It will have its healing effect upon you."

This man's letter told of the place he visualized. It was his grandfather's farm in the Catskills where, as a lad 50 years ago, he used to drink at the spring, swing in the old-fashioned swing under the apple tree, slide down the cellar door, and "holler down the rain barrel." There he could see the mountains outlined against the sky and smell the aroma of hay in the loft. "I had not been there for years," he wrote me, "and had had no communication from there. As I mentally visualized the old farm, I seemed to see workmen tearing down the old homestead. I told my wife of this strange occurrence. She telephoned relatives in that community, and was told that the exact scene I had described was actually taking place. They *were* demolishing the old house, to install that citadel of progress, a gasoline station, on the site."

How can we explain this strange phenomenon? I maintain that this man was there in his mind, in the essence of his soul, in the deep perception of his personality. How else could he have seen it in exact detail?

So when in deep moments you want to feel the touch of Jesus Christ upon you, yield to Him, believe that He is there, affirm that you feel the touch of His hand upon you, feel the secret of His presence. Trust in Him. You will not only be *thinking* about Jesus Christ, you will be *with* Jesus Christ.

I have seen too many evidences of His presence to have any doubt. When He said, a long time ago as recorded in Matthew 28:20, "I am with you always, even to the end of the age," He meant it. Exercise your faith and ask Him to touch you, your fingers, your heart, your control switchboard, which is called the mind. He will give you strong discipline and control, so that you can deal with your nerves in a positive manner. And you *can*, if you will practice living with Jesus Christ, day-by-day.

The second exercise I suggest is akin to the first; that is, practice being calm. Whatever the circumstance may be, get yourself to the point where you do not move quickly. Quick movement is devastating. There are times, of course, when you must move quickly. But for the most part, don't! Be quiet and calm under all circumstances. Emphasize calmness in your thoughts and you can achieve a calm reaction.

Late one night, I was in my apartment all alone. It was about one-thirty in the morning and I was sitting in the library working. There wasn't a sound, except for the usual far-away noises of the city. Suddenly, I had a most terrifying experience. Loud, clear, and penetrating, a single note was sounded on the piano in the next room. I could feel chills running up and down my back. I projected myself out of my chair like a pilot who has just been ejected from a jet plane! But for once, I practiced what I preach.

I sat back in my chair quietly and said to myself, "If there is a stranger in this place, he would not be so foolish as to sound a note on the piano. He might bump into it, he might sit down on the keys and hit many notes together; but not one single note." I reasoned with myself as calmly as I could. Then I walked cautiously into the living room and looked around. I went to the piano, and sitting on the keyboard, looking at me with a bland and innocent expression, was the family cat.

And my now telling you about this brings back to me the feeling of mastery that surged through me, at that moment when I was startled. This is a foolish illustration, but on some dark night of the spirit when you hear sinister noises and witness fearful appearances, remember to believe that He is with you. Be calm; keep your nerves under control for the emergencies that may arise.

The author Victor Hugo wrote, "When you have accomplished all that you can, lie down and go to sleep. God is awake." That is beautiful, is it not? A friend sent me a story about a woman who went to her doctor complaining of being in a highly nervous state. The doctor was a Jewish refugee whose family had been killed in Germany. He said to her, "I know full well what you mean by nerves. When you lie down in your bed at night, get yourself a motto and put it up on the wall where it is the last thing you will see before sleeping. The motto should read, 'Good-night, worries. I will see you in the morning.'"

There is one final exercise I suggest. Physicians tell me that sometimes a tumor will develop that impinges on a nerve. An operation is performed that is called a nerve-block operation. Certain sections are blocked off until the offending growth is removed.

As serious as this sounds, I would a hundred times rather have a growth in my body impinging on my nerve, than a "growth" in my mind impinging on the great trunk lines that lead to and from my nerve-control switchboard. The growth to which I refer is made up of guilt, sin, and wrongdoing. No wonder some people are nervous and tense. Look what they are carrying in their minds. They were never meant to allow a foreign element to develop at the control center of their lives.

These people go to doctors and psychiatrists trying to find peace, when all they need to do is go to the Great Physician, and have a little operation performed whereby such malignant soul growths are removed. I have known people to carry these moral growths for years. I am reminded of an old, white-haired man who came to me one time for such an operation. I performed it in my spiritual operating room and sent him out a healthy man. "How long have you carried this sin?" I asked him. And how long do you think he had? Fifty-two years! And under such tension, he had repeated this sin a few times during those years!

There is another man who used to come to New York to see me frequently. He would sit down and say, "Doctor, I've listened to your tapes, I've read your articles and your books, and I go to church wherever I am. But I do not get peace of mind. Everything makes me nervous; my business, my son's escapades, the government. I can't sleep, I am always under tension. I am a nervous, bottled-up, unhappy person."

Finally, after many visits, I said to him, "I have known

you for a while, now. I am sure you are a reputable citizen at home. What is it, really, that makes you so nervous?"

"I don't know," he answered. "I want to find out."

I took a long shot and said, "You and I are close friends. I am a minister and that makes me a confidant. You can tell me anything and I will never reveal it. Talk to me as if I were your brother. You need not be ashamed."

And he did. He got it all out, though he was quite embarrassed. And believe me, it was quite a lump of stuff.

"How in the world," I asked him, "did you ever expect to live at peace with yourself, when such a load was impinging on your mental switchboard? Now," I said, "Jesus Christ can take a nice, clean knife and cut all around that growth and take it out. Then fill the void with the presence of Jesus Christ: that is our healing balm."

This happened a long time ago. And though he contacts me frequently, he has never again talked to me about being the victim of nerves. He is still as active and hardworking as ever, but he carries himself with imperturbable poise and there rests upon him a great calm.

If a sin you have committed is causing you great anxiety, get it forgiven. You do not need to go to anyone and tell him as did the man I have just described.

All you need to do, right now, is shut your eyes and tell Jesus Christ about it, telling Him you are sorry for it and asking Him to forgive you. If you are committing any sins now, for the sake of your health and happiness and peace of mind, stop it. If you do not have the strength to stop it, turn to Jesus and tell Him you want to live under His control, and let Him touch you; for when He lives with you, you will not go to some of the places you are now going, you will not meet some of the people you are now meeting, you will not be thinking some of the thoughts you are now thinking. You will have changed your whole life.

Is He not wonderful?

Anxiety is the great modern plague. But faith can cure it.

—Smiley Blanton, M.D.

CHAPTER 8

Develop Your Full Potential

For God hath not given us the spirit of fear; but of power, and of love, and of a sound mind. —2 Timothy 1:7

IT is wonderful what we human beings can do with ourselves when we set our minds to it, if we believe and trust in the power of God, and work at it. When we gets into harmony with the creative power of Jesus Christ, there is no limitation we need to place on ourselves. We are infinitely perfectible! This is one of the great teachings of Christianity; and it is good ole American doctrine. It has been expressed in many ways, but never more eloquently than in this passage from the Bible: "For God hath not given us the spirit of fear; but of power, and of love, and of a sound mind" (2 Timothy 1:7).

There is a friend who, for many years, was filled with conflict, haunted always by disbelief in himself. He did only fairly well in his work. At the age of 50, a time when the average person is supposed to be past hope of change, this man became humble and childlike. He went to a wise counselor who explored his personality. He talked freely, explaining his desires, defeats, hopes, and fears. He was given a series of aptitude tests. Today, he is in a business for which he had no previous training. He is running a chain of attractive and successful restaurants. He has conquered his feelings of defeats and, at the age of 57, has achieved one of the most successful personality victories I know. Whenever I talk with him, I am astonished at what a human being can do to change himself by following certain fundamental laws. I like to stress this faith in change because people are always asserting that, while this change may be possible to some, it is not for them.

One summer, I spoke at an agricultural convention. That visit was one of the high spots in my experience, for I discovered what can be done with non-human nature, with livestock. One man compared the cattle brought over by our forefathers to this country with those we have now. Another speaker dealt with chickens. You wouldn't think a speech about chickens would be illuminating, would you? I was so astonished that, later, I spent an hour in the chicken exhibit. I learned that 276 varieties have been developed. These impressive birds held their heads erect, deeply conscious of their breeding. They were tremendous, and believe me, they knew it.

A third speaker discussed the laws of scientific culture as applied to livestock. I was thrilled. I know this sounds foolish but, after that meeting, I went to see my friend, a farmer who has developed some of the finest chickens and livestock I ever saw. He is a scholar and scientific farmer. He even plays music to his hens and, whether or not that has anything to do with it, he gets top egg production.

Since that convention, I have been asking myself why we allow science, with all its deep understanding and skill, to develop the finest hogs, fowl, and cattle in the world, but do not apply these same laws to the highest form of God's creation, the human being, in whom there is resident such marvelous potential. Man was given dominion over everything; yet he, himself, is dominated by his weaknesses and his conflicts. He lives constantly in the midst of failure, discouragement, and evil. How pathetic this is!

I hope the desire for self-improvement has not died in you. I sincerely trust that you have not arrived at the time when you are willing to take yourself as you are and put up with yourself until the end of your life. It is a bad state of affairs when one allows his spirit to sink. Pull yourself up! Get the thrill of making yourself better than you are! There isn't a single human being who cannot overcome his weaknesses, resolve his conflicts, sharpen his mind, expand his capacity, and live an amazing life.

How do we go about doing it? Based on what I have seen people do, I would like to suggest the following methods. In the first place, we must consider our attitudes. William James, the great American psychologist, has said, "Human beings can alter their lives by altering their attitudes of mind." If you have an attitude of fear, hesitancy, shrinking, or inner conflict, then life will give you back fear, hesitancy, or conflict. If you will immerse your mind in the mind of Jesus, you will get a wholesome respect for yourself and will be filled with love and goodness.

Years ago, I met a man who was upset. He had just been made an officer in his company, and he had to meet with the president every day.

"That man's effect on me is overwhelming," he confided to me. "I am literally frightened to death. I can't think when I am in his presence. He is extremely capable, and I have a terrible inferiority feeling. If I could get over that, I know my chances for advancement are good. But I think I shall have to resign, for I find myself going to pieces from fear and nervousness. What shall I do."

"I don't know," I said. "Let us ask the Lord. Let us pray about it. 'For God hath not given us the spirit of fear; but of power, and of love, and of a sound mind.' You know that." So we prayed.

Finally I said to him, "When the president calls you into his office, stand at the door before you enter and pray for him. Don't pray for yourself—you must forget yourself. Send out thoughts of love to him." And I added, "His very pomposity may be an indication that he needs love and understanding; someone not afraid of him. Pray that, when you talk with him, you may be a help to him, that a wonderful relationship may develop between you. Then open the door and go in."

"I'll try," he agreed.

When I saw this man again, he was a different man. There was a sense of power and happiness about him.

"How are you getting along with the boss?" I asked.

"He is the most wonderful man I have ever known," he said. "When you get by that rough exterior, he has the kindest heart in the world. He is almost like a father to me, and has given me some wonderful suggestions. Not long ago, he said to me, 'Bill, I have come to depend on you. You are a wonderful help to me.'

"Do you know that is the greatest thing that has ever been said to me. All of a sudden," he finished excitedly, "I felt like a new man."

What had happened? His attitude had changed from one of self-consciousness and fear and tension to one of love and relaxation.

The next suggestion is one I have made so many times that you may think I have become a fanatic on the subject. But I am going to say it again. The average person uses only a small percentage of his potential power. I have heard the claim made that most of us use only 20 percent of our brain capacity. How do we increase this percentage? In the Bible, Jesus always talks about faith; always talks about optimistic visualization; always talks about affirmation; always talks about people as the children of God. He constantly helps people develop this super-consciousness, this extra potential we all have.

I recall a man who often came to our church in a wheelchair. He was more agile in handling that chair than many people are on their feet. He had been in that chair since he was 17, when he was crippled by rheumatic fever. His family was poor. His mother and father both worked, leaving him alone, sitting in his chair, saying to himself ceaselessly, "Useless, useless, useless."

Then, one day, he said to himself, "I am not useless." He picked up the Bible and began to read. Finally he was saying to himself, "So what, if I have no leg power, no arm or hand power. I have a sound mind. There is nothing crippled in my mind."

He continued to read; and the Bible told him he had soul-power. "I can't run like other guys. I can't use my hands well. But I can use my mind and my soul with the best of them."

He finally figured out what he could do. He decided that he could make greeting cards. With his gnarled and crippled hands, it took him a week to make the first card. And he suffered indescribable pain. But he sold the card— at a profit. Today, he has a company making these cards by the thousands.

You can do anything with your mind, if you want to

do it bad enough. But people assume they haven't any power. They say to me, "I am sixty, I'll have to retire; there isn't anything for me to do; I am through."

In one speech, I began with a quotation from William Shakespeare. I forgot the words of the quotation and filled in with some lines of my own, and finished with Shakespeare. Someone from my audience challenged me afterward.

"You didn't quote Shakespeare correctly," he said.

"You know too much." I tried to smile.

"Oh, well," he consoled me, "anyone is bound to forget when he gets to be your age."

I was indignant. "Who's getting old?" I demanded.

"You can't remember so well when you're over fifty," he explained.

I don't agree with that gentleman. The reason a person takes the attitude that his mentality is slipping as he grows older is because he thinks that is the way he is supposed to be. Why kill yourself off before the Lord takes you?

I was talking with a friend about this subject of memory. He told me he had people more than 80 years old in memory-training courses, and that they passed their tests with a high degree of accuracy. I asked him to give me a memory test; and I won't tell you how I did on it. But he outlined for me how a person can have a wonderful memory. Here are some of his ideas:

First precept: Never say you haven't a good memory. On the contrary, say, "God, in His goodness, has given me a marvelous memory."

Second precept: When you meet anyone, use your powers of concentration. Suppose you are meeting me. Afterward, perhaps, you will remember my face, but not my name. Why? Because you look at my face, but only half hear my name. Then you go around saying, "I can remember faces; but I just can't remember names."

Focus, advises this memory expert, on the powers of concentration. "When you walk along the street, and see an automobile license plate, look at it; then shut your eyes and see if you can remember it. Also, learn a passage of Scripture a day." And finally, he says, "Say to yourself all the time, 'I have tremendous power within myself.'"

We do have tremendous powers within ourselves. A writer needed more money than his publisher was willing to give him. He had an imaginary conversation with the publisher, reminding him of the good books he had produced, insisting that he ought to be paid an increased rate. The publisher advanced arguments which, mentally, this writer demolished. The conversation ended, "I expect you to pay me the rate I am asking."

Several days passed, and the writer tried to steel himself to call on his publisher and put the rehearsed conversation into use. But before he could do so, his publisher called him. "I have been rereading your earlier works," he said, "and I am impressed with the way you have grown. I have decided to pay you more than what we originally agreed on," and he mentioned the figure the writer had decided upon in his own mind.

There is tremendous power in the human mind. Of course, these incidents might be criticized on the ground that they are physiological maneuverings to bring power out of the personality. But naturally, the greatest of all personality improvement comes from surrendering to, and cooperating with, the spirit of Jesus Christ. Preaching is the greatest job in the world because, no matter how poorly you do it, you are telling people that, if they yield themselves to Jesus Christ, wondrous power will be given them to improve their personalities.

Just what this is, I do not know. Just how it operates, I cannot diagram. But I have seen it happen too often to leave any room for doubt. When a person seeking improvement turns to Jesus Christ, he finds indeed a scientist beyond description.

In one sense, nature seems to confer special privilege upon some people, endowing them with genius and gifts of greatness and success denied the rest of us. But it remains true that even though men and women are sometimes given these gifts, unless they exercise and develop them, they cannot improve themselves, they cannot attain success. It is also true that some lesser persons whose gifts are in small measure—one talent instead of three— can attain what some three-talent people fail to achieve.

No one in any kind of position can succeed unless he loves his job. Now, you may have a job that you don't love. You may hate it. Why? You may say to yourself, "I hate this job because it is too demanding." You may say to yourself, "I'm stuck in this job because the job market is tight and there are no jobs out there for me." But if you do leave your current position for another, you will often find the same difficulties, or worse ones. Before you go off and make a change you might regret, first try to learn to love your job, whatever it is. Love it with your mind first. Think about your job objectively and positively, not negatively. But if yours is one of those rare cases where you cannot love your job, then find one you do love. Loving your work and being enthusiastic in it is one of the fundamental factors in successfully improving yourself.

One summer, I happened to be associated with people in the movie industry. I met one of the greatest actresses of all time, Bette Davis. I told her that I often speak to young people, and young people are interested in getting ahead, and improving themselves.

"What is your idea of success and the secret of your own achievement?" I asked her.

In her own quick manner, she replied, "I am an actress, but I make no pretense of being pretty. I do know," she said, "that I love to act. I could get up in the middle of the night to act. I simply love it. You are a minister— don't you love to preach? If you don't, you should not try to preach. We must love our jobs." She was vibrant, and there was a light on her face as she spoke. When the call came to go back to work, she went with eagerness and delight.

If you are a secretary, you ought to love it. It's an art to write a good letter. I know, for I have seen some bad ones. Think of what you can do for the people you meet. A business person who is discouraged comes into your office. Business is difficult and life is hard. A kind and sympathetic word from you can make his whole day different.

But you don't love your job. You sit in front of your computer with a deep dissatisfaction inside. You hate the place and everyone in it; you hate yourself, too. So you fail and everyone who touches you fails to the degree to which they touch you. Love your work. Put into it the infection of enthusiasm. Give people a lift by your spirit. Say with enthusiasm, "I love to do what I am doing," and that will help you improve and become successful in any line of activity.

Another way you can improve yourself is never to let

yourself become discouraged. Let nothing defeat you. We sometimes look at people who have succeeded and wonder how they did it, often not realizing that they did it by never giving up. Your job may be difficult. You may have those two strikes against you, so what are you going to do? Will you give up without a fight? Oh no, you're not going to do that. There's too much in you to do that. There is enough fight in you to keep you going. You have got in your soul the power of God. Say, "If this is the right thing to do, I will do it no matter what goes against me, or how tough things become. I will never weaken and I will never give up. 'For God hath not given me the spirit of fear; but of power, and of love, and of a sound mind.'"

It is no coincidence that the last four letters in American spell, "I can." —Peggy Germain

CHAPTER 9

Expect
A Miracle

He that believeth on Me, the works that I do shall he do also; and greater works than these shall he do.   —*John 14:12*

CHRISTIANITY is something tremendous. Too often it is presented as ordinary, but don't you ever believe that! When it is reduced to the commonplace, that is tragic, for the message of Jesus is electric, dynamic, and vital. It is packed and supercharged with power. It is bursting with hope!

If you think I'm overstating the case, let me quote a passage from the 14th chapter of the Gospel of John, the 12th verse: "He that believeth on Me, the works that I do shall he do also; and greater works than these shall he do." That is quite an offer! Think of the power and the hope contained in that passage.

What did Jesus do? He made the blind see, the lame walk, the sick well. He raised the dead. He changed the world. And He said to His followers, "If you believe in me, the great things that I have done you shall do." And He even goes on to say, "And greater works shall you do than I do." Such a statement may be difficult to conceive, but there it is right in the Bible.

I believe in the Bible. I have read it and followed it for years and have never known it to give me bad guidance.

It has the answers; you can depend on it. The Bible makes it clear that every human being can do infinitely more with himself than he has ever done.

But so many of us do not really appreciate or realize our potential. Your life doesn't need to be dull or ordinary. Every great thing Jesus did, you can do, *if* you believe. You can work miracles in your life. And any group of people, such as a nation, for example, can work miracles.

This country, by believing in such a power, can become a greater nation than ever before. It is not necessary for our nation to be as uncertain and mixed-up as it is. One reason why it is in the present situation is because too many people have abandoned God and fundamental moral values. In 1788, the English historian Edward Gibbon completed his classic, *The Decline and Fall of the Roman Empire,* in which he listed five reasons for that fall:

1. The rapid increase of divorce: the undermining of the dignity and sanctity of the home, which is the basis of human society.

2. Increasingly higher taxes and the spending of public money for free bread and circuses for the populace.

3. The mad craze for pleasure; sports becoming every year more exciting and more brutal.

4. The building of gigantic armaments when the real enemy was within, the decadence of the people.

5. The decay of religion—faith fading into mere form—losing touch with life and becoming impotent to guide the people.

A recent poll conducted by *Who's Who Among American High School Students* found that an overwhelming majority of the nation's brightest teen-agers admit to cheating in school. Publisher Paul Krouse concluded,

"There is a real breakdown in the ethics of our young people." Lew Armistead of the National Association of Secondary School Principals said: "The headlines are full today of examples of unethical behavior by some of the most prominent people in this country. The kids are seeing that and reacting to it."

First, we read one survey that tells us that teen-agers are religious and approve of having prayer in the public schools. But then we see another survey that says the majority of teens surveyed admit to cheating on exams.

How can this be so? Young people apparently have a natural religious inclination, but something happens when there's a moral decision to be made. Why study and work hard, when you can cheat and get the same results? Maybe it's "cool" to cheat, so your friends won't think you're a nerd. But what will happen to America, if we raise a generation of young people who will follow the crowd, not standing up for their moral convictions? Or do what's easy, instead of what's right?

If this nation returns to God, it can work miracles. We have been fed a weak, insipid Christianity for too long. Our Christian faith is tremendous. Any nation can work miracles, if it gets back to believing in the greatness of God and what He offers.

Some of the ideas for this chapter came to me while riding on an ultra-sophisticated train called "The Romance Train." It runs between Tokyo and Nikko in Japan, a distance of about 90 miles. Most of the trains in America have deteriorated but, in many foreign lands, there are marvelous trains, including this one in Japan. The service includes a hot towel to cleanse your hands and face, delicious tea at no extra cost, attractive attendants to watch over and serve you. It's real red-carpet treatment! There is nothing like it in this country.

The Romance Train starts from the Tokyo station, goes through the suburbs, and finally reaches the high country around Nikko, home of one of the great shrines of Japan. Going through the outskirts of Tokyo, I was impressed by the vast number of industrial plants, the size and quality of which are a symbol of the great industrial development of Japan. And the names over those plants are now world famous! All this is evidence of the economic and industrial production and distribution in Japan that now rivals that of the great United States itself!

And Tokyo, a city of more than 11 million people, larger than New York City, is infinitely cleaner and safer! Great, towering, beautiful buildings and huge networks of highways make up this prosperous city. The streets are filled with orderly, well-dressed people; no bizarre, way-out costumes such as you sometimes see in other parts of the world. Most Japanese men wear a dark suit with a white shirt and a necktie, and the girls wear skirts.

The residents of Tokyo are a thoughtful people. You get a sense of dynamism as you realize that, not too many years ago, Tokyo was almost completely destroyed; it lay in rubble, absolutely prostrate and bankrupt. But the people took their losses philosophically; they believed in the future; they got to work with energy, and an astonishing miracle—a great thriving metropolis has risen from the ashes of destruction. I've been there several times. Every time I go back, I have to say that there is no city in the world quite like it.

If you can make a great, clean city out of rubble, why can't you make a great, clean city out of one that has never felt a bomb? Miracles can be performed by human beings, if they believe, if they plan, if they work, if they tackle difficulties philosophically.

Believe in the future; go to work with energy. And in our philosophy, the great Christian faith, we have Jesus Christ to help us, if we fully accept Him and trust in Him. "He that believeth on Me, the works that I do shall he do also; and greater works than these shall he do." Can you imagine what could happen in this nation if we really practiced Christ's teachings, and went for them wholeheartedly? It is there, all right. All we have to do is take it.

And just as a nation can change, miracles can happen in individual lives and people can become altogether different. As they themselves are changed, these changed people change situations; for they get hold of the great concept that it is possible to work their own miracles.

How do you go about doing that? Number one is to get hold of one word. One word does it, a magic, dynamic word. A miracle always begins in the mind, and if you insert this word into your consciousness, the miracle will begin. The word is *possibility*.

Reject the impossibles; dwell on the possibles. Be a possibility thinker. Consider any question by stressing the possibilities, not the impossibilities. The possible stands out like a great, shining light above the skyline of dismal clouds. Get that bright word out there among those clouds—*possibility*—and you will be amazed how the sky begins to clear. No matter how difficult things are, no matter how hopeless, no matter how dark, keep the word, *possibility*, firmly in your mind.

One evening, Mrs. Peale and I left Honolulu at ten o'clock on a non-stop flight to New York City, 5300 miles in 9 hours and 2 minutes, which is what you might call a little rapid. It was a beautiful flight. As we took off from Honolulu, seeing the romantic island slip behind us in the blue-black Pacific, its lights fading in the darkness, the captain told us that in 3 hours and 48 minutes, we would pick up landfall over a little town north of San Francisco. And I wanted to see landfall.

But I became drowsy and soon went to sleep. However, I'd set my mental clock to wake me up at landfall and, believe it or not, it worked. When you're flying east at night, of course, you soon run into dawn. It was the beginning of daybreak when I awoke and saw the mainland of the United States extending into the ocean.

The Coastal Range was discernible, but the great mountains were lost in morning mist and fog. As we swept over the coastline, I saw the top of a mountain, a great, tall, cone-shaped mountain, covered with snow from its summit to as far down its sides as I could see. It was perfectly silhouetted against the mist and the fog.

"It can't be Mount Ranier," I said to myself, "we're too far south; it can't be Mount Hood, either. It must be Mount Shasta." I asked the flight attendant to check with the navigator, and he said it was Mt. Shasta. I have seen this mountain on many occasions, but never like this. The sun was bombarding its eastern face, turning it into gold and pink and all the bright colors of the morning. It stood resplendent in all its glory, pushing its great cone up above the mists, above surrounding mountains. It was an unforgettable sight.

As I followed the mountain until the great engines of the plane obstructed my view, I sat there thinking that you could apply the word "possibility" to Mt. Shasta.

However dark it is, however hopeless, however despondent, there is possibility like a great, lilting, searching, upthrusting pinnacle of purity and light! So, get the "Shasta" possibility on the skyline of your life. You will work your own miracles.

"Well," you may say, "that Shasta illustration may be poetic and beautiful. But when you get right down to the nitty-gritty, how do you go about working a miracle in your life?" Let me tell you about a famous actress who faced a difficult situation. On a television program one day, I heard her make a marvelous statement, "A winner never quits and a quitter never wins." I listened for a few minutes to get the relativity to the statement.

The speaker was Rosalind Russell, and she told of her struggle with arthritis. When she was a little girl, her father repeated that dynamic statement over and over again: "A winner never quits, and a quitter never wins." Rosalind Russell testified that when crises came in her life, she remembered that advice and it worked. She overcame many things, including a battle with arthritis that almost crippled her. But she would never accept defeat. She expected a miracle and she got it!

Just what is a miracle? It is a phenomenon we cannot explain by scientific formula, but which can be explained by the spiritual formula of positive faith, of possibility thinking. Never accept anything but the possible; never think the impossible. If you believe in Jesus, the great things that He did shall you do.

This is a wonderful theme, a terrific theme. My enthusiasm for it, and my belief in it, are so great that I want you to accept it. I want to put it across to you. If I could be more persuasive, maybe you would say, "That is terrific! That is great! I know it is the truth. There will be no more impossibles in my life. I'm going to put the possibility principle to work in human affairs." All you need to accomplish that is to have some faith: *Believe* it. Whoever believes will have belief come to pass. Miracles happen in people's lives, if they believe.

When Mrs. Peale and I were in Tokyo, we had dinner with some friends, Mr. and Mrs. Peter Sawada. Peter had attended Marble Collegiate Church when he was in the States. Now that we were in Japan, he and his wife wanted to take us to dinner. We had a typical Japanese dinner, which I always find delicious—and non-fattening, too—a wonderful meal! After dinner, we went back to the Sawada home, a typical Japanese house where you take off your shoes at the door. During our visit, Peter told us about his father, now deceased. But the impression left by the father upon his son is quite profound.

This is the story: As a boy, Peter's father, the son of a poor fisherman, lived in the mountains of the island Hokkaido. Meanwhile, in Hanover, N.H., a young man became thrilled with the idea of bringing Jesus Christ to the people of the Orient. So he traveled all the way from Hanover to the Japanese city of Tottori. There was no railroad to Tottori; to cross the mountain range, he rode in a rick-shaw, a man-pulled cart. It was a two-day trip, with a night spent at the mountain pass before descending to the small city. But he finally arrived and spent day after day preaching to the people. The little boy listened to him, and the boy's father, Peter's grandfather, listened to the missionary, too.

One day, the missionary was called to another section of Japan. The father said to the little boy, "Son, that missionary has something that is different."

"Yes, Father," the boy replied, "and I believe in him. I want to live the great life he talks about."

So the father said, "Son, this is what you will do. Cross the mountain and find the missionary. Sit at his feet. Learn all that he has to teach."

As Peter continued with the story, he said, "We Japanese have a custom of bringing a gift, so my grandfather gave my father a beautiful, wooden tea container, decorated in the Japanese style. And with this gift in his sack, he crossed the mountain pass to find the missionary."

When he found him, he said, "Sir, I've come to sit at your feet. I want to know more about your teachings," and he gave him the beautiful tea container.

The boy, Peter's father, became a good pupil. He learned about Jesus Christ and believed in Him. The missionary helped him get an idea of the outside world. He became one of the leading men of Japan, Ambassador to France, Ambassador to England and, finally, Ambassador to the United Nations.

When Peter's father arrived in the United States, he went to Hanover, N.H., to see the widow of the missionary. She was now a gentle elderly lady who welcomed him into her home.

They sat together and reviewed old times. He told her how much he had loved her husband, how much he loved her, and how his whole life had become a miracle because of the teachings of the missionary.

"Son [for he'd never grown up, in her mind], I want to show you something." She went to the mantlepiece and took down a beautiful red wooden tea container, decorated in the Japanese style. "Do you remember this?" she asked. "My husband cherished it and told me to keep it always, ever to remind us of a little boy, son of a poor fisherman, who listened and who believed, and who worked a miracle in his life."

In the dynamic, creative name of Jesus Christ, go out and work your own miracles. "He who believes in Me will also do the works that I do; and greater works than these will he do."

The smallest deed is better than the grandest intention.

—*Larry Eisenberg*

CHAPTER 10

Shape Your Future

*But as many as received Him,
to them gave He power to
become the sons of God.*

—*John 1:12*

A NEWSPAPER article reported that 94 per cent of Americans surveyed said that they were merely enduring the present so that they might reach the future. I had no idea there were so many people in this country in such a miserable state of mind. Whether it is actually so, I wouldn't know. But I do know that, in the human mind, the future is full of hope and promise.

The past is often discolored with unhappy memories and we gladly walk away from it. The present is full of responsibility, difficulty, struggle, and sometimes pain, and we have trouble living with it.

But the Lord has provided a future where the past may be forgotten and where the present may be eased, where our highest hopes and dreams and anticipations may come to realization. It is a great land to which we travel—the bright and glorious land of the future.

This future is ever impinging upon us; it is just one step ahead of us. Your future is extraordinarily important. So how can we go about improving it?

This question, like most every question, has an answer

in the Bible. That is why the Bible lives. It makes no difference what problem you have; you hunt through this Book, and you will get your answer. What is strange about it is that this Book is just as adequate in our complicated, sophisticated times as it was when it was first written, in an age of camels silently traversing the floating, drifting sands of the desert.

In the Book of John, the first chapter, twelfth verse, are these words, which are the formula for having a glorious future: "But as many as received Him, to them gave He power to become sons of God." In other words, to those men and women who accepted Him, took Him into their lives, and built their lives around Him, He gave the power to become something—to have a fine future. Take Him, receive Him, and all our weaknesses will fall away; you will overcome your frustrations, your defeat, your ineptitude; you will have the power to become.

I once talked with a teen-aged boy who had an enormous inferiority complex. He was shy, reticent, shrinking—defeated by everything. He had told himself ever since he was a child that he was inferior and life was terrible for him. He lived in the Midwest.

One September, he went to the county fair. Now you wouldn't expect to get any life-changing results at a county fair, but you never can tell!

There was a woman at the fair in exotic Oriental costume. For five dollars, she would tell your fortune. He thought maybe she could tell him what was to become of his miserable life, so he submitted himself to her treatment. She took his hand and said, "I am impressed as I look at your palm. There is a long life-line. You are going to live a long and wonderful life."

126

Then the fortune-teller said, "I see other lines in your hand. Here is one that indicates you are a natural-born extrovert."

"Oh, no, madam," the boy replied, shyly. "I'm an introvert."

"As I read the mystic lines in your palm," persisted the fortune-teller, "I know you are an extrovert."

The boy left the tent walking on air. He passed all the side-shows, saying to himself, "What do you know? I'm not an introvert; I'm an extrovert. I'm not inferior."

Then he went to a religious conference for young people, a conference that was built around real commitment to Jesus Christ. And this boy, who had begun to look at his possibilities, had a terrific spiritual experience, and began to look at what the future could be.

Our potential is tremendous. There isn't anyone who could not do a better job in life than he now is doing. But we are inhibited by our narrow-minded attitudes and our lack of trust and faith in God, and in ourselves.

How about you? Are you going to crawl through life on your hands and knees, piteously saying how difficult everything is? Take a long look at the potential that the Almighty God has built into you. You will discover that you can do tremendous things with yourself. You will discover that you can find true meaning in life, real personal inner organization.

It is true that life sometimes deals defeating situations, situations over which we have little control. The only control we have over them is that we will not, by the grace of God, be mastered by them. The pity of it is that we defeat ourselves by our attitudes. Your conscious mind tells you, "I am defeated. I am weak. I am inadequate." Those are dangerous things to say, because your subconscious mind is always listening to your conscious mind, always trying to oblige you.

How pathetic it is that people, by a mental process, actually make themselves into exactly what they don't want to be! But how glorious it is that, also by a mental process of faith, you can make yourself into precisely what you want to be, with the help of God!

I was a guest on a television-talk show where people call in and ask questions. They see you, but you don't see them, although you do hear their voices. A man called in and said to the interviewer, "This question is for Doctor Peale. You, Doctor Peale, are always talking about positive thinking. Let me tell you something: You're dealing with a case, right now, where that positive thinking of yours just won't work."

We were not off to a good start. He was saying that he had a question for me but, no matter what my answer, he knew it wouldn't work. "I'm fifty-eight years old and out of a job. You know as well as I do that it's pretty hard to get a job anywhere at fifty-eight. And you know as well as I do that, in our area, employment is at a low level. So I am absolutely hopeless.

"In the next place, even if I did find a job, it wouldn't be the kind of job I want. And even if I did get the job I want, I don't have what it takes to handle such a job. And," he concluded, "no one likes me." One negative statement after another.

"Well, my friend," I replied, "do you insist on being this way, or do you really want help?"

"I want help," he answered.

"What you need is a treatment in *psychogenesis*," I said.

128

Although I wasn't really sure of the exact definition of psychogenesis, it sounded impressive. Actually, I did know that it meant, by the very name of it—*psycho* and *genesis*—that everything begins in the mind. "What you've got to do, in my humble judgment, is to get a whole new frame of mind," I told him. "I'm not on this television show to preach a sermon, but I'm going to do it anyway.

"I want you to look up this statement in the first chapter, twelfth verse of John in the Bible. It is, 'But as many as received Him, to them gave He power to become the sons of God.'" And I gave him a little explanation of it. Then I said, "Meditate on that text throughout the day and, when you go to sleep at night, drive it into your subconscious.

"Next, tell yourself, 'I am a man fifty-eight years old. By reason of that fact, I must have some wisdom. I have great experience and know-how, and I am at the peak of my manhood.' Say that to yourself and you will become convinced that you indeed have possibilities. And also say, 'Unemployment in this area isn't that bad; there is a place for me.' And then say to yourself, 'I am an adequate person, and everyone likes me.' And you might add to that, 'Besides, I now like myself.'"

"Let me write those things down," the man said. And we delayed the whole show as he wrote down what I had said, checking with me as he wrote. I prayed for him quietly, and I thought about him from time to time, wondering if he had found himself.

Some months later, I was giving a speech at a business convention. And this man came up and reminded me of that incident.

"Are you that man?" I asked, in surprise.

"I sure am," he replied enthusiastically.

"Are you connected with this convention?" I asked.

"Sure am!" he answered cheerfully.

"Have you a job that you like?"

"Sure do!" he said. Then he added, "But you and I really didn't have anything to do with it."

"You're right," I agreed, "but tell me who did."

"Why," he said, "you know it's that wonderful Jesus Christ. He is the One. Isn't He astonishing?"

To as many as received Him, to them He gave the power to become. The way this comes to pass is that you receive the power to improve yourself—and by improving yourself, you improve your future.

A great many people have only an obscure, fuzzy notion of what they want their future to be. They want to go somewhere, but they don't know where they want to go. Well, you will never go anywhere, if you don't know where you want to go.

Imagine going to an airline-ticket counter and saying to the person, "I want to go someplace."

He asks, "Where do you want to go?"

You say, "I don't know, but I want to go. I want to get somewhere."

The person would be disgusted. You have to say, "I want to go to Indianapolis" or "I want to go to Cleveland." When you tell him you want to go to Cleveland, he is able to give you a ticket so you get on the right plane—one that goes to Cleveland, not Los Angeles.

This may sound silly, but it really is important. Often it happens that some man or woman, having come to me for counseling, has complained of never getting anywhere. I ask, "Where do you want to get?" And sometimes, the answer is that the person just doesn't know. Well, how can you get where you want to go, when you do not know where you want to go?

Nothing of great value in this life comes easily. The things of highest value sometimes come hard. The gold that has the greatest value lies deepest in the earth, as do the diamonds. So if you want glorious tomorrows, you must want them with all your heart.

There is a story about some ancient philosopher to whom there came, one day, a mere boy, saying, "Master, I want knowledge."

The philosopher asked, "How much do you want knowledge?"

"Oh," the boy said, "I *really* want it."

"Well," remarked the sage, "to get knowledge you have to want it as you want nothing else." And he continued, "You just come with me."

He took the boy to the seashore, where together they waded out until they were in water up to the boy's chin. Then the philosopher put his hand on the boy's shoulder and pushed him under the water. For a long moment, he held him there, kicking and squirming and struggling to be released. Finally, just before the drowning point, he let him up. Back on the beach, the philosopher asked, "When you were underwater, what did you want more than anything else in the world?"

"Master, the thing I wanted more than anything was air," the boy answered.

"Well," said the older man, "when you want knowledge as you then wanted air, you will get knowledge."

Now, the Bible tells us that to those who receive Him, Jesus gives the power to become the sons of God, which means to have serenity, love, compassion, goodness, and strength. But, of course, there is a lot of evil in us. And to know yourself spiritually, you must face and know the evil that is in you. This is a phase of self-discovery that everyone should enter into. There is a great deal of evil in the human heart, and it gets down into the unconscious and motivates much of our lives. We are sometimes directed almost entirely by it. And if one wants to really know himself and get freed from his limitations, he has to uncover this evil that is in him.

Now, it is one thing to gain a future for yourself, as I have indicated. And it is another thing to build a future for the world. And to do that, believe that the future of the individual is in Christ and the future of mankind is in Christ. What is the trouble with our world today?

It comes down to one thing. Of course, secretaries of states and foreign ministers and politicians will give you long speeches on what is wrong with the world; but they are just people like the rest of us, trying to do their best, doubtless, but caught up in the old political game of power against power, equating this with that. Basically the trouble is just this: evil against good. The reason the world is in such a troubled state is because of the power of evil. And evil isn't in the air; evil is in men's hearts.

Well, we are God's children, and we are supposed to be creative. It is time for us to do something about the world problem. We must first realize that good is more powerful than evil. Then we must individually rise to the challenge. Each must say, "I will be God's man" or "I will be God's woman," and "I will put a healthy spiritual life against the evil of our time." With enough people doing that, we would see the dawn of a golden age.

One of the greatest passages in the Bible is in the sixth chapter of Isaiah. It begins: "In the year that king Uzziah died . . ." Uzziah had been a great king; he was dead. "In the year that king Uzziah died I saw also the Lord sitting upon a throne, high and lifted up, and his train filled the temple. Above it stood the seraphim . . . . And one cried unto another, and said, Holy, holy, holy, is the Lord of hosts: the whole earth is full of his glory . . . . Then said I, Woe is me! for I am undone; because I am a man of unclean lips, and I dwell in the midst of a people of unclean lips . . . ."

In other words, there was disintegration and decay all around. And Isaiah heard the Lord asking, "Whom shall I send, and who will go for us?" Now Isaiah didn't respond by suggesting that the Lord send the prime minister, send the secretary of state—oh, no. This is one of the glorious passages of Holy Writ. He answered, "Here am I; send me."

If you want a future for yourself, your children, and the world, *you* go out and do something about it. What can you do? Get yourself so full of the transforming power of God and Jesus Christ that you are infectious, electric, dynamic, and an influence for spiritual health. That is the way the future comes to human society.

"Here am I, Lord, send me." Each day, get up and look in the mirror and say, "The future—my future and my children's future—depends on me." Not on you as a weak creature of flesh and blood, but on you inhabited and filled and overcome with Jesus. The future depends on Him. He creates a future through you and me. Your future and mine and the world's depend on what we are. And what we are is what will come. So remember that to as many as receive Him, He gives them power to become sons of God.

Never be afraid to trust an unknown future to a known God. —Corrie Ten Boom

CHAPTER 11

Wish Wisely

Now unto Him that is able to do exceeding abundantly above all that we ask or think, according to the power that worketh in us. —Ephesians 3:20

ON a surf-washed, sun-kissed beach in Florida, I had a thrilling conversation with one of New York City's most successful business leaders. I call it thrilling because it was the story of what a Christian and an American can make of himself, if he so wishes. It is considered old-fashioned, in some quarters, to pay tribute to the American story of how a man or a woman can start at the bottom and, by dint of perseverance, character, and the freedom under which he or she lives, climb to the top.

As a boy, this man lived in the Tennessee Mountains. His father was an itinerant preacher who, with his family, subsisted mostly on the produce given him by his parishioners. Twice a day, through the town where they lived, a great express train thundered without stopping. It was a flier, headed from the great cities of the East down to the cities of the South.

This boy used to sit on a baggage-truck at the station, listening to the long, low whistle of the train reverberating in the hills and watching, fascinated, as it roared by. The men sitting on the observation platform of the train seemed to this boy obviously captains of industry. And he would sit and dream of the time when he, too, would ride by in that observation car. The little Tennessee hillbilly, as he called himself, made up his mind to do something big in the world.

"Most of my dreams were without foundation and they crumbled," he said. "But with the help of God and the freedom of the United States, I was able to put a firm foundation under some of them." Then he added reflectively, "There is more to this wishing business, this dreaming business, than appears on the surface."

Again and again you hear the phrase, "I wish!" It is usually poignantly, pathetically said; a tacit admission that a wish is a will-o-the-wisp, an unrealizable attainment. "I wish!" But as force is the basis of physics, so is the realizable wish the basis of psychology, an intricate part of faith. There should be, indeed there is, a procedure by which we can build foundations under our wishes, by which when a man says, "I wish," he releases creative power.

When I searched for a text for this theme, I found a wonderful one: "Unto Him that is able to do exceeding abundantly above all that we ask or think, according to the power that worketh in us" (Ephesians 3:20). That is to say, Almighty God will give you not only abundantly, but exceeding abundantly, more than you ask, more than you have ever thought about.

That is extreme generosity, is it not? Ah! But there's a catch to it. It continues, "According to the power that worketh in us." In other words, you can obtain what you wish for *only* to the degree to which the power of God works in you. Life will give you wonderful things, says the Scripture, to the extent to which you are filled with

God's power. That being so, how do we go about the art of successful wishing?

First, you must analyze your wishes, because it is a subtle truth that sometimes what you think is your wish is not your wish at all. There is a basic wish in your mind. It is something you would rather do than anything in this world, something you would rather be than anything else. But people sublimate their wishes and are constantly striving for that which they do not really want at all.

Not long ago, an industrialist installed in his plant a department for studying the aptitudes of his employees. As a result, they have been taking a lot of round pegs out of square holes. Under the old system, people were hired for whatever job was open and many of them were doing things they were not cut out to do. Now, they are analyzed and placed in the jobs best suited to their ability and temperament.

One man was determined to be a sales executive, if it killed him. By dint of overwhelming toil and much talk, he worked himself into that position and was a complete failure. The aptitude test indicated that he was better suited to working in the accounting department. He is there, now, and is extraordinarily successful.

As a boy, he loved figures and financing. Why had he wanted to be a sales executive? Because all his life, all his intimate friends had been salesmen. So he had the notion that that was the greatest job in the world. He thought it was his basic wish, but it was not. Without realizing it, his real wish was to be an accountant. And when he got into accounting, he was a great success.

I remember a boy who wanted to be a preacher, so in college he studied for the ministry. Later he had a church and did not seem to do too well with it. He asked me to listen to him preach, but I declined, as I did not want to judge him. It requires a good deal of presumption to tell a man whether or not he should stay in the profession he has chosen.

He was later offered a fine position in business, a position of many opportunities with a salary 15 times greater than he was getting as a preacher. This might have tempted him, but he did a powerful lot of praying against accepting it. Then I went to hear him preach, curious to see what kind of sermon brought him such an offer. In the pulpit, I found him with an entirely different personality. He was halting and slow, and his sermon was colorless and lacked aliveness.

"What should I do?" he asked me later.

"Pray about it a little more," I suggested. "You know the church needs fine laymen who can make money, because we have to continuously raise money to meet expenses. You can serve as a layman with the same devout consecration you have given to the ministry, and you will know exactly what to do with that fine salary."

He took the job. And when I was raising money for the church, I shall never forget the splendid contribution I collected from him. He was happy from that day on. His personality never changed again; he has remained the same wonderful person I had known.

Why had he wished to be a minister? His grandfather had been one, his uncle had been one, and his father; and now his brother was one. His mother told him from infancy that she had dedicated him to God and the ministry—which of course she had no right to do. She could dedicate him to God, but she was wrong to tell him what his life's work should be. So he thought that was his wish; but his real wish was to be a capable man of business.

You must discover by analysis, by thought, and by prayer, what is your real wish. You will never attain it unless you are working for what you really want. When you do, you will find that He is able to do for you exceeding abundantly beyond all that you ask or think.

Then you must have a proper wish. When we pray, we say, "This I ask in the name of Jesus Christ." That means that, whatever we have asked for in prayer, we don't want unless it is in accordance with the will of Jesus Christ. An improper wish can never bring you any good; it can only bring you harm. If you will test your wish according to the principles of Christ and the will of God, it will bring you magnificent results.

A few years ago, an executive vice president of a firm came to see me about a business matter. His wish was to build up his business to the greatest in its field.

"A man in my organization stands in my way," he began. "He has known me since I was a baby. My father put him in the firm. Now my father is dead, my uncle is inactive, and I am running the business. But this old gentleman doesn't treat me with proper respect. He tells everyone I'm just a kid, that I don't know anything, that I should be in the nursery. I've decided to fire him."

"Have you fired him?" I asked.

"I thought I would see you first," he answered.

"How long has he been with you?"

"About forty years. He's now sixty-six years old."

"Of course, you're planning to give him a nice pension, aren't you?"

"Why should I? He's always had a big salary. We have

no pension system. If he hasn't saved, it's his hard luck."

"How old are you?" I asked.

"Twenty-two."

"If you are so determined about firing this man, why did you come to me."

"I thought you'd tell me it was all right. It would ease my conscience."

"Let us pray about it now," I suggested. "We'll ask the Lord if this is a proper wish. Then you go about your business and I will pray about it several times between now and tomorrow afternoon, Sunday. Then let's return here and see how we come out with our respective prayers."

The next day, we met again.

He said, "Well, you were right."

"What was I right about?" I asked.

"It would not be right to fire him. I will talk with him and tell him I have to be head of our business. But as he is an old family friend, he and I will work it out together. He's a smart man and knows the business better than I. He might keep me from making bad mistakes. It is curious, but that's what came up in my prayer."

"That is what came up in mine, too," I answered.

I heard no more about the matter until this letter arrived. It begins:

> You will be interested to know that everything is going along smoothly and the solution you helped me achieve apparently is permanent, inasmuch as our conference on the subject took place nearly two years ago. I'm delighted to say that things have worked out well. I hope you may convince more businessmen and women that these principles really do work in practical application.

I happen to know from another friend that this man's business has had an astonishing development under the combined management of this young man and the older man. His improper wish, if persisted in, might have destroyed him. But by thinking of "Him that is able to do exceeding abundantly above all that we ask or think" and according to the power that was working in him, he became an artist in successful wishing.

First, be sure of what you really wish. Don't deceive yourself. Second, always see that it is a proper wish. Then there is another important factor. One of these days, we will learn the value of the technique of visualization. Visualization means to take a wish, check it to see if it is a basic wish, check it according to the rule of God to see that it is a proper wish, then hold it as a picture in your mind. Visualize it. See it already accomplished. See its form and structure as already built. There it is. It is built in your mind; built in your heart; built in your prayers. You have checked it. You know it is your basic wish. Now, hold it there.

I know a husband and wife who were poor. They were city people, but had been country folk. It is a curious thing about the American today. The average man works his head off to get to the city, where he labors long and hard so that he can hurry back to the country!

But the feeling he has of going back is not the same as when he came from the country. He wants to return as a gentleman farmer, for the country is in his bloodstream and cannot be stilled. He likes the thrill of the city, but he also likes the cold look of a brilliant, starlit night in winter. He likes to feel the sidewalks under his feet; but he would far rather hear the crisp snow crackling beneath his tread, as he tramps along the country lanes.

These two people worked hard and lived in one room. At one point, they lived with their in-laws, where they used to huddle over a radiator and dream it was a huge fireplace. Every night they prayed, "Lord, help us to move into our dream house in the country." They had it all pictured in their minds. Finally, they acquired a car and, on Saturdays, they went looking for their dreamhouse.

One day, they saw it on a hilltop. It looked just like the blueprint their minds had held, but the real-estate agent in the community told them the people who owned it would never sell.

Five years passed before they were finally able to buy it. They were about 40 years of age on the day they took possession. The moving van was in the driveway. They got out of their car and walked up the steps hand-in-hand. He carried her across the threshold and, in one of the vacant rooms, they got down on their knees and thanked the Lord who had given them this basic wish, who had given them a proper wish, who had pictured it for them. As a result of this visualization, the home was now theirs.

Are you asking, "Can I get something like that?" One time I told a similar story and a man wrote me a letter. "You know very well," he said, "I can never get anything like that."

I wrote back, "You are dead right. You don't want it. What you want is failure. You have the will to fail." This man was rationalizing his failure, criticizing me for saying he could realize his dreams. You can get anything Almighty God wants you to have and it is far beyond anything of which you now dream.

"But," you say, "this is materialistic, wishing for a

house." I don't know if it is! People have to have houses, don't they? Where do you draw the line between the spiritual and the material anyway?

However, be sure that what you want is right—a basic wish. There is nothing stingy about God. He is always talking in generous terms. "Him that is able to do exceeding"—that is a marvelous old word—"exceeding abundantly above all that we ask or think,"—but there is a catch to it—*"according to the power that worketh in us."*

If you will allow yourself whole-heartedly and absolutely to be filled to overflowing with the power of God through Jesus Christ, there is nothing in the way of a substantial wish that is not realizable. This is the art of successful wishing.

No dream comes true until you wake up and go to work.

—Banking

CHAPTER 12

Always Be an Optimist

If any man be in Christ, he is a new creature: old things are passed away; behold, all things are become new.

—2 Corinthians 5:17

WE live in a time of great affluence. But apparently, there are more emotionally and mentally miserable people than we have ever previously had in the United States. While he was research director of the Rockland State Hospital at Orangeburg, N.Y., Dr. Nathan S. Kline asserted that there is more human suffering from depression than from any other single disease.

Another doctor has said that each year in this country four million patients take antidepressant pills to get their moods and spirits under control, and approximately six million others are constantly taking tranquilizers to ease their agitated mental states. Each year, there are thousands of recorded suicides, thousands more that do not become known, and perhaps several hundred thousand attempted suicides—and this in a land where there is more wealth, more opportunity, more abundance than in any country in the history of the world.

What's come over us? What's gone wrong with us? We need a new birth of the philosophy of optimism.

At regular intervals, we need to make a frontal attack

on the pervasive gloom that periodically permeates this country. Today, we seem to be enshrouded with pessimism and uncertainty. Let us get rid of this gloom and depressiveness in the name of the only one who can lift the shadows and let in the sunlight, namely, Jesus Christ our Lord.

Not since 1929 have I seen so much negativism. One newspaper reported that well over half of the people interviewed consider that the problems we face in this country are getting worse; some even predicted that it would go on like this for many years to come.

Well, I don't buy that at all. The situation today is infinitely *better* than it has been in the real bad times. And that isn't taking an unrealistic view, either, because we know of the difficulties many people face every day.

But it appears that the economists cannot tell us exactly how to correct the situation, even though they are supposed to be wise men and women. White House officials proclaim that the economy has turned the corner and is finally on a path of steady recovery. But many economists say it is far too early to declare victory over the economic downturn.

So who is telling the real story? Should we be pessimistic or optimistic? Since they haven't any answer, I thought I'd try one myself! Of course, I am no economist in any sense of the word. But I have had some experience throughout the years in dealing with gloom and depressiveness. And when such an attitude falls over the entire public like a plague, it is time for someone to come up with a solution for creating a better situation.

When he heard that I was going to talk on the powerful effect of optimism, a young friend of mine berated me. "In the first place," he said, "optimism is silly. And in the second place, if you want to find optimism, the church isn't the place to find it." He then described the many dull, sleepy and (to use his words) dopey preachments he had heard in church. When I pressed him, I found he hadn't been to church in a while, but still he had an image of tediously dull sermons.

I asked my friend where he *would* look for optimism. "Maybe you'd go seek it among the bright lights of Broadway?" I suggested. Now, some of those lights *are* bright, there *are* good plays; but on the other stages, sad, mixed-up, conflicted characters drift in a shadowy haze for three hours before audiences that have spent up to $100 to hear talk about nothing.

Similarly, we have many fiction writers who publish sad tales. They grope for some solution to life; but they know no solution, so their characters go through all manner of mix-ups and come out still mixed up.

I asked my friend, "Where *would* you look for optimism? And why don't you find it in your New Age philosophy? You seem to have a tired view of life. You're so sad always. Why are you so sad?"

"Because life *is* sad," he replied.

Well, life does have plenty of trouble in it. It is full of dark, deep, grievous trouble. And Christianity recognizes this. The reason Christianity survives as a philosophy is because it faces all of life, including all the evil thereof and all the wickedness in man; it paints the whole picture but, nevertheless, affirms that, in the midst of all this trouble, pain, and confusion, there is a good outcome, there is a lilting something that sings its way out of sorrow. The bright, pure lily comes up through the mud.

There had never before been a philosophy of human life like Christianity. It realistically deals with all of the hardships of the human condition, but it comes out with victory. That is because of what is in its essence.

At the heart of Christianity, there is a great, splintery, blood-splattered cross. You can't laugh off the pain and the sorrow and the suffering of life. But the lilting note of victory is never absent. That is why it was said of the early Christians that there was something in them akin to the song of the skylark and the babbling of brooks.

Optimism, hope, freshness, newness. One text after another speaks to us of these: "If any man be in Christ, he is a new creature: old things are passed away; behold all things are become new" (2 Corinthians 5:17). Again: "Walk in newness of life" (Romans 6:4). And again: "I saw a new heaven and a new earth: for the first heaven and the first earth were passed away" (Revelation 21:1). New, new, new. Freshness, newness. That is Christianity in its essence. Newness.

There is no day so beautiful as a day in early spring—unless it be a day in October, or a day in summer, or a steel-etching day in winter; we love them all. But there will come that first day of spring, not according to the calendar, but because of new life. You'll look out some morning and see diamonds of dew in the grass. The robins will sing and the sky will be clear and the air will be balmy, and everywhere around you will be newness of life. You'll walk along feeling, *Isn't it good to be alive? I feel new.* There is also a springtime of the spirit, which is constant, in which we walk in newness of life. And it comes to those who practice the powerful effect of optimism.

There was an event in New York City that used to be

called the Fulton Street Prayer Meeting. It began back in 1859, when there was in this country what was then called a panic, which started in 1856; now it is called a recession. Money was in short supply; the stock market was at the bottom; business was bad; all the economists were consulted and none of them came up with a solution.

There was a man named Lamphier who was a member of Marble Collegiate Church those many years ago. He worked as a clerk in Wall Street. He was a devout Christian who believed in the power of prayer. As things went from bad to worse on Wall Street, he decided to hold a prayer meeting.

He sent out a notice that there would be such a meeting at noon on a certain day and every day thereafter. He arranged 20 chairs in a circle in his office and waited for others to join him. That first noon, no one came, and the meeting consisted entirely of Mr. Lamphier. So Mr. Lamphier prayed.

The next noon, a few came; the following day, several more joined in; by the end of the week, the room was filled. Following that example, prayer meetings sprang up all over New York. The movement spread to Philadelphia, to Baltimore, to Washington, to Chicago, and throughout the nation. It gave rise to one of the greatest spiritual revivals in the history of this country. In connection with it, the economy rebounded. People began to think positively; they began to believe; they went to work. And this combination of prayer and action led the United States into one of its highest periods of material and spiritual prosperity.

The lesson learned here is that optimism is a powerful influence. And it can work wonders by setting loose an amazing resurgence of Christianity that affects the whole social order. When optimism and faith go together, a wonderful thing happens in people's lives.

Now what is optimism? Well, before we answer that question, let us ask what pessimism is. Pessimism is a philosophy that holds that the evil in life overbalances the good in life.

Optimism, on the other hand, is a philosophy based on the belief that basically life is good, created and sustained by a good God; and that, in the long run, the good in life overbalances the evil; also that, in every difficulty, every pain, there is some inherent good. And the optimist means to find that good.

So optimism isn't some cheery, Cheshire-cat, moonlight-and-roses philosophy at all. To be a true optimist, you must be rugged and tough in mind. No soft person can be an optimist. An optimist is a person who believes in a good outcome, even when he can't yet see it. He is a person who believes in a greater day, when there is no evidence of it. He is one who believes in his own future, when he can't see much possibility in it.

"Well," you say, "I'd like to be optimistic, but I have a lot of dark clouds in my mind all the time. I see nothing but the gloom and the hardship and the pain and the suffering. It's all very well for you to talk so enthusiastically, but what am I going to do with all these clouds? I have a low ceiling."

Many people do live under a low ceiling. Why not go out and take a few plane rides and see what a low ceiling really amounts to? Up above the clouds, there is always the sun shining. Down here, on earth's surface, groping around in the shadows under a low ceiling, a person may not feel optimistic. But you should begin to practice the optimistic upthrust. Send up into the mass of dark clouds bright, powerful, optimistic thoughts and optimistic faith. By doing so, you can dissipate the clouds and have an entirely different life. Send up constantly into the overcast shrouding your mind bright thoughts of faith, love, and hope; thoughts of God, thoughts about the wonderful greatness of life.

Optimism, when it is applied to our lives, cleanses the mind of unhealthy thoughts. And, of course, unhealthy thoughts quickly take away the joy, the peace, and even the health of life. An injection of Christian optimism will rejuvenate the entire social order.

I don't know whether or not I can convey this, but there is an ecstasy possible to human beings that most of us miss. And in missing it, we miss the best of life. Recently, I read an article by Dr. Abraham Maslow of Brandeis University, a well-known psychologist. In the course of studying average, healthy-minded people, he has found that many such persons tell of having experienced "moments of great awe; moments of the most intense happiness or even rapture, ecstasy, or bliss." Dr. Maslow thinks buoyant health in itself frequently gives rise to feelings of great joy. How many moments of great joy have you had? That it is an interesting question.

The poet Walt Whitman wrote, "To me every hour of the light and dark is a miracle." The author Robert Louis Stevenson wrote, "To miss the joy is to miss all." The poet Edna St. Vincent Millay exclaimed, "O world, I cannot hold thee close enough!" Paul Tillich, a theologian, tells us, "Where there is joy, there is fulfillment, and where there is fulfillment, there is joy."

And to the person who consistently practices optimism there comes joy. But this will never come about unless we prepare and discipline our minds for living at these levels. Yes, I know it isn't easy. But I maintain it is worth all the effort—and this you know when glorious experiences of life in its essential beauty come upon you.

Strange the way these things happen. My wife, Ruth, and I were in a Tulsa, Okla., hotel one night. I was lying in bed, when all of a sudden I heard a glorious sound. It was a sound I had thought no longer existed in the United States. But I distinctly heard it: The sound of a steam locomotive, pulling westward out of Tulsa on the Santa Fe. And it whistled at some crossing, with that old steam whistle. Then it whistled again, presumably at the edge of town. I lay there listening. I heard it whistle again off in the ring of hills, almost lost in the distance—the long, low, mournful, romantic sound of a steam whistle.

And suddenly I felt inexpressibly happy. I was traveling back in memory to my boyhood days, when that was a romantic sound. But the experience went deeper than that. It seemed that everything around me was alive. And I felt a surge of life—and then, apparently, I dropped off to sleep, which seems curious. If I were so alive, why did I? I guess it's because of tensions giving way.

The next morning, the sun was streaming in the window of the hotel room. I walked around and looked out at the Arkansas River and the prairies, and I had one of those intense awarenesses of how good life is, of how happy I was, of how I loved everything—the world and everyone in it—and how I loved life itself. It was so overpowering that I could hardly contain myself.

I asked my wife if she knew why I was so happy. "Well,"

she said, "maybe those whistles you heard last night were what did it." Then she said, "No, that isn't it. You feel His presence, don't you?" And I did. I could hardly contain myself for joy.

Now, we couldn't live in such ecstasy all the time. But to know that that's what life is in its essence, and to believe in it through the dark moments and the hard days, this is optimism. And you develop this optimism by thinking it, by acting on it, and by practicing it.

A friend was telling me about his mother-in-law. She was a nice lady, he said, but she got all tired out by eight o'clock in the morning. And she wasn't even out of her bed by then.

"How could she get herself all worn out?" I asked.

"Well," he said, "she lay there thinking of all the terrible things that were going to happen to her, how badly everything would turn out, how many problems she had, how many difficulties she had to face—and by eight o'clock, she was so tired she could hardly get out of bed."

This kind of thinking can tire you out and affect your whole day. Henry David Thoreau used to lie in bed before rising and tell himself all the good news. And upthrust the thought of it into the overcast.

But there is a secret deeper than this. I have discovered that the most optimistic people are the most Christian people. Now, I've got to qualify that a little bit. I have seen laymen, preachers, bishops, archbishops, and so on up and down the hierarchy who weren't optimistic, who thought everything was going bad. You see, there are different ways of being a Christian.

A minister in London told me about a man who never would go inside a church. But he would hang around in the vestibule. And when the ushers went away, he would open the door just a crack so he could listen. But he would never venture further than the vestibule. Well, there are many who physically have got past the vestibule, but, mentally, they're still listening through a crack. They're only getting a tiny bit, a faint suggestion of the Gospel. But Jesus said, "Drink ye all of it" (Matthew 26:27).

If you take the whole of Christianity and really give yourself to it and really accept it, you are going to become so happy, so enthusiastic, so optimistic, that life will be altogether different for you. Then you will walk in the newness of life—when you have absorbed the quality, the essence, the depth and the height, the glory and the power of Christianity.

So let go of that gloom, let go of that depression, let go of that discouragement, let go of that weakness, let go of that sense of failure. Get yourself with Jesus—really, personally. Go to Him, pray to Him, tell Him you want to live with Him, tell Him you want to be guided in your life by Him.

And I will guarantee, on the basis of everything I have seen happen in my ministry, that you will become optimistic; you will become victorious; you will have peace in your heart; you will love people; you will feel good physically and emotionally. You will have a wonderful life.

*There's no danger of develop-
ing eyestrain from looking on
the bright side.* —Cheer

CHAPTER 13

Give Your Best to Others

Jesus saith unto him, Rise, take up thy bed, and walk.

—John 5:8

A BUSINESSMAN wrote to me: "We have a man in our employ who has been with us for many years. He is capable and well trained; we need him, he needs us, but he has lost his grip. He doesn't get along well with his associates. He is drinking too much. Something has gone wrong with him. I'd like to help him. What can I do?"

Another recent letter read: "There is a couple in our group whom we all love; fine people, both of them, but they can't seem to get along with each other. And it looks as though their marriage might go on the rocks. How can we help them?"

Here is a third letter: "George is a wonderful boy, comes from a good family, 16 years old, has had every advantage. He is in a wild crowd. Recently, George was caught stealing. Yet he has no need to steal. No one wants to see this boy a confirmed delinquent, but no one seems to know how to reach him. How can we help?"

So runs a good portion of the mail that comes to me. And, no doubt, there are few of us anywhere who cannot think of people we would like to help, if only we felt adequate to do so. What, then, can we do about it?

Of course, there are experts in helping people—psychologists, pastoral counselors. But there are too many problems, and not enough experts to go around. Besides, every Christian person should be a creative individual, with resources for helping others. Christianity is not meant just to help you or me, but to help us help others. And in helping people, Jesus can be our model. For Jesus is the wisest, keenest, most astute, most scientific, most skillful helper of human beings who ever lived. To confirm this, all you need to do is read the New Testament.

Take, for example, the incident at the pool of Bethesda (see John 5:1-9). The word "Bethesda" means "bubbling spring." This particular spring is located in Jerusalem and I have seen it. In Jesus' time, the pool of Bethesda was near the sheep market, and around it were five porches. On those porches lay all kinds of sick people, waiting for an angel to stir the pool.

According to tradition, whoever got into the pool first, after the water was stirred, would miraculously be healed. Jesus came to this place, and He took notice of a certain man who had been lying there 38 years. Because he had been there longer than anyone else, this man enjoyed a good deal of prestige. He was the oldest of the old-timers at the pool.

Jesus went up to this fellow and said, "Would you like to be healed?" Now, He knew that the man did not really want to be healed, because he was enjoying a lot of self-pity the way he was—self-pity and prestige.

The man replied, "Yes, I'd like to be healed, but you see how it is. When the water bubbles, there is never anyone to come put me in the pool and, before I can get there, someone always gets in ahead of me."

Now, you'd think, wouldn't you, that in the course of lying around there for 38 years, there would have been one time, at least, when he could get in first. You would think, if nothing else, that he could inch up to the edge of the pool and, when the water bubbled, just flop right in. But no. "There is never anyone around to help me." Many people are like that. They don't really want to be helped.

Jesus knew that the man was fooling himself, that he had built up a barrier of self-pity and was hiding behind it. Jesus went up to him and looked him in the eye. He asked again, "Do you want to be healed?"

And the poor fellow lifted his feeble eyes and looked into the eyes of Jesus. Power was transmitted. Perhaps he saw reflected in the eyes of the Master that which he could be, and for just one minute, the manhood that he originally had had came forth, and he said, "Yes, Sir, I would like to be healed." And that was all that was necessary.

Jesus said, "All right, pick up your bed and walk away from this place."

The man looked at Him in disbelief.

"I said, pick it up. Do it yourself." And the man took up his bed and walked away.

So often I hear people say they would like to be healed of their fears, their hates; they would like to be healed of this or that weakness or frustration or discouragement or ineptitude. But do they really want healing? That is the question. If you look into the eyes of Jesus and say, "Yes, I want it, I really mean it," wondrous healing can take place.

To help other people, we must study them, we must know them, we must look behind the facade they have built up. We must develop understanding. Human nature is complicated, quite devious. But you can understand it by prayer, by study, and by love. Love is the greatest teacher in the world. If you love anyone well enough, you will begin to understand him. And with this there develops patience. Understanding, love, patience. With these three, you can help another person. Sometimes all that is needed for being helpful is to transmit a sense of patient, understanding love.

My friend Arthur Gordon, a writer, tells a significant story about a man he knew. This man was a newspaper editor in a small town. He was often at his desk until late at night, writing his editorials and doing other work. One night, around midnight, there was a rap at his door. He yelled, "Come in!"

The door opened and there before him was the haggard face of a neighbor, a man whose little boy had drowned recently. The editor knew the circumstances. This man had taken his wife and son out canoeing, the canoe had overturned, the wife had been saved, but the child had drowned. The man had been walking the streets in a daze.

"Here, Bill," said the editor. "Sit down and rest."

The man sat, slumped in utter dejection. The editor continued working. After a while he asked, "Would you like a cup of coffee, Bill?" He poured him coffee. "Drink that, old boy. The warmth inside you will do you good." They sipped their coffee. No conversation.

After half an hour of this, the neighbor said, "I'm not ready to talk yet, Jack."

"That's okay. Just sit there as long as you want. I'll go on with my work."

Much later, Bill said, "I'm ready to talk." Then, for a

solid hour, he poured it all out. He went over the tragedy in meticulous detail—what actually happened, what would have happened had he done this, what would not have happened had he not done that, in every detail blaming himself for everything. By three o'clock in the morning, he was rundown and tired. He stopped talking and said, "That's all I want to say tonight."

The editor went over and put his arm around him and said, "Go home, and get some sleep."

Bill said, "May I come talk to you again?"

"Anytime," the editor told him. "Whenever you want to, day or night." He slapped him on the back and said, "God bless you, old boy."

The editor gave his friend no counsel, no advice, no suggestion. He didn't feel competent to do so. He gave patience, love, and understanding.

In the last analysis, every man and woman on this earth has to solve his own problems. But you can help people if they can come to you as one who understands, who loves, who is patient, who will stick by them, who believes in them, who shares with them.

Take you business people, for example. You have people in your places of business who have all kinds of burdens and problems. Do you let them talk to you? Or do they shy away from you? Are they afraid of you? Or do you have no time? You have daily opportunities for helping people, for much can be done by just letting them talk.

I had an interesting experience some time ago aboard ship, crossing the Pacific on the way home from the Far East. The first day out my son, John, said to me, "Dad, there's a man on this ship who has no use for you."

"Well," I said, "that wouldn't surprise me, but how do

you happen to know this?"

Well, it seems that John and some of the young people had been playing deck tennis and then had gone to the Marine Veranda—a fancy name for the cocktail lounge—the only place they could get soft drinks. Here they sat, drinking soda pop and cooling off.

"There was a fellow sitting at the bar, an American, and he was drinking one whiskey after the other," John continued. "There was no one else around and he was talking to the bartender. I was talking with the other kids when, all of a sudden, I heard your name. This man was saying to the bartender, 'I don't give a blankety blank blank blank if Norman Vincent Peale is on this ship. I'll drink all the whiskey I want and Norman Vincent Peale can go blankety blank blank.' Whoever that fellow is, he sure has no use for you, Dad."

"Well," I said, "it would be interesting to know why."

The next day, as we were having lunch, a stranger came over to our table and, in a very gracious, pleasant way, said to me, "I beg your pardon, Doctor, but I want to introduce myself. I'm Mr. So and So. I'm having a party in my cabin before dinner tonight. The captain is coming and some other people, and I would be honored if Mrs. Peale and you would join us. Will you?

Well, I wasn't filled with any burning enthusiasm, but the man looked like a nice fellow and his manner was kindly. So I said, "All right, we'll be there."

As soon as the man was out of earshot, John said, "That's the guy! That's the one who was cussing you out to the bartender."

"You don't mean it!"

"Yes," he said, "it is. You'd better watch that fellow."

Well, I went to the party. My host asked me, "Doctor, what will you have to drink?"

"Have you any Seven Up?"

"Oh, yes, we have lots of Seven Up." So he gave me a Seven Up, and he took one, too. Now, friends, I like Seven Up, but one is enough; yet I drank three Seven Up's with this man. Nicest fellow you ever saw in your life.

The next day, I met him on deck. We walked around together. The man was good company. I was increasingly puzzled about the outburst John had overheard at the bar. It was hard to believe this was the same person.

Suddenly, the man said to me, "Doctor, I want to ask you a question. Why has God got it in for me? He has done me a terrible thing. I don't like what He did to me."

"What did He do to you?" I inquired.

"I had a wife. For twenty-seven years, we were married. I loved her. She was everything to me. My whole life was built around her. God gave her cancer, and then took her away from me. Why did He do this to me?"

Then I saw what was wrong. This man was hurt. He was bewildered. He was angry.

"I'm drinking a lot," he continued. "I don't like myself this way. But why did He do it to me?"

We talked a little. I asked, "Do you go to church?"

"No," he said. "I used to go to church every Sunday with my wife but, now that she is gone, I don't feel like going to church by myself. I would just be sitting there thinking about her."

I told my wife, Ruth, about all this. She went to the man and said, "Mr. So and So, I have a problem. I never can sit with my husband at church services because he is always up front. Would you sit with me on Sunday?"

That is what you call spiritual strategy!

On Sunday, I looked at the congregation, and there sat my wife with our acquaintance beside her. He was singing the hymns. He seemed to know them, too.

And in the days that followed, we were able to do a little work together on all that pain and anger in his heart.

Now, why had this man been cussing me out before he had ever met me? You see, had he cussed God out to the bartender, the bartender wouldn't have stood for it. So he had to create some kind of symbol. I happened to be a minister, and therefore connected with the church, and the church is connected with God. So I was a convenient symbol upon which he could unload his hate. There was nothing personal in it.

We must learn to question why people do the things they do, why they say this or that. We must learn to be objective. If a person says something about you, say to yourself, "Why did he say that? There must be a reason." Be objectively scientific about criticism. It may be your opportunity to help someone.

Look up into the eyes of the Great Physician who asked, "Do you want to be healed?" First, get healing for yourself, so that you may be full of patience, understanding, and love. Then give of your best to others, by what you say, by what you do, by what you are. And you will enter into the wonderful experience of helping people.

Those who bring sunshine to the lives of others cannot keep it from themselves.

—James Barrie

CHAPTER 14

Make Every Day a Good Day

This is the day which the Lord hath made; we will rejoice and be glad in it.

—*Psalm 118:24*

IS it possible to make every day a good day? Some people will respond by saying that it is simply not possible that every day should be a good day.

Well, let me ask you this: Are you absolutely sure that it cannot be so? Is it just because you think it cannot be so? Or is it, perhaps, that basically you don't want it to be so? Is it possible that you have become one of those negative persons who get a certain enjoyment out of their own misery? That, of course, is characteristic of the human mind at times. But it is my belief that we *can* make every day a good day, with God's help.

I have always been interested in the writings of the late Charles F. Kettering. He was, in many respects, one of the greatest practical researchers in the country. As head research scientist for General Motors, for many years, he was truly a genius. It was he who developed the self-starter for the automobile, and the process of painting automobiles with spray guns. He also researched many other new developments.

Kettering never took anything for granted unless it was definitely proven and, even then, he would sometimes hold that it might be unproven. At the time of his death, he was working on the question of why grass is green. He said many people had told him that grass is green because it is green. But he wanted to know why it is green. Why isn't it pink instead of green? I am sure he was sorry he couldn't work that one out before he died.

Well, he made a statement some months before his death that impressed me greatly: "The trouble with a great many people is that they know too many things that are not so." That is to say, people all too often get notions they are sure are true, when actually, under scientific scrutiny, they may not be true at all.

Now, I do not mean at all that every day can be an easy day. Nor do I mean that there is not going to be for, each of us, lots of pain, disappointment, and suffering in life; but we are so endowed that we can take all these things and make good days out of even difficult ones. There is nothing soft about life, but neither is there anything impossible about it. My conviction is that, if with all your heart you truly seek Jesus Christ until you find Him, and really take Him into your life, you can make every day you live a good day.

The late Governor Wilbur Cross of Connecticut was a real positive thinker. He would say to his family at breakfast, "It's a good day for it." He did not specify for what. But the family knew that the Governor expected it to be a good day for whatever. All who were accustomed to his attitude believed it would indeed be a good day. I'm sure that Governor Cross had his share of tough days, of sorrow and disappointment. But his attitude of expectation about the days of his life must have paid off in the majority of times he called out: "It's a good day for it!"

I remember when I first saw my lifelong friend Judson Sayre as he came to college. He was a poor country boy from the backwoods. I liked him at once and so did everyone, for he had personal qualities that were to take him to the top in business. Jud became one of the greatest salesmen of his time.

I stayed with him in his elegant apartment on Lakeshore Drive in Chicago. I said that night, "Jud, you certainly have made a great success of your life. How do you explain it?"

"Come into my bathroom," was his surprising reply.

"This is where I shave every morning," he said, pointing to something pasted on the mirror.

"Read it out aloud," he said.

> Think a good day
> Thank a good day
> Plan a good day
> Put God into it
> Give it all you've got—get going.
> Start and end the day with God.

Jud was one of those big-souled, lovable men who are really religious from childhood training, but are sort of backward about revealing it, seeming to be soft-like. For example, he didn't talk about God. But he would occasionally say, "I talked to Jesus about it."

Recently at an airport, a big, fine-looking African-American man came up to me and introduced himself. He said, "I want to bear testimony to you about the power of God in a human life." What a wonderful man he was! He stood at least six feet, six inches tall. I had to look up to talk with him. And he had the most marvelous smile.

He continued, "Since I found the Lord Jesus Christ and took Him into my heart, I have not had one single bad day." I asked how long that had been, and he told me nearly two years. "Don't get the idea," he said, "that I haven't had my troubles. During that time we've had sickness in the family and several crises in our business. But when you have Jesus Christ, there is such a lifting power that it raises you above all these things."

I stood there looking at him and thought, *This man certainly has got it.* I said, "You know, you remind me of a text from the Bible."

"What's that?"

And I quoted this passage from the 24th verse of the 118th Psalm. "This is the day which the Lord hath made; we will rejoice and be glad in it."

"Ah," he said, "that sure is it."

Every day can be a good day. When the Lord created the world, He created a firmament, He created the waters, He created night, He created day. After He had finished His creation, He looked upon it and saw that it was good. It is man who has made the days bad. If you have bad days in your life, God didn't do it; and don't try to say that that is just the way it is. That is the way it isn't.

We make most of our own bad days. Every difficult day I have ever had, I made myself. True, I have associated with some people, now and then, who sure helped me make them bad! But if I had applied the true spirit of Christ, I could have risen above even that.

There is quite an art to being a Christian. It takes genius; there is nothing little about it. No wonder it is said that Christ is for the strong. Weak, flabby, undisciplined people can't really live Christianity. Do not let that trouble

180

you, though, for when you give yourself to Him, you become strong.

All day, this very day, and tomorrow, are precious segments of time that can be made wonderful, one after the other. And how should we go about making them so? Psychologists have said that the first five minutes at the beginning of the day, as you awake from sleep, and the last five minutes of the day, as you fall asleep, are extraordinarily important, because then the mind, the consciousness, is in its most malleable state.

The first five minutes of the day should be dedicated to God. The person who takes the first five minutes of conscious thought and fills it full of God, will condition himself or herself for the entire day. We have all heard the old saying, "He got out on the wrong side of the bed this morning." What side of the bed you get out of has nothing to do with it, literally; but your mental attitude as you get up is important. What we expect, we are likely to get. Expect a bad day and you are likely to make it a bad one, right from the start.

One of the greatest artists of this country was Howard Chandler Christie. I once asked, "Howard, give me the secret of your health and happy spirit."

"Well," he replied, "I start every day by filling my mind for fifteen minutes full of God." Then he added, "Nothing bad can get in when it is packed full of God."

I was talking once with a woman of considerable force who told me, "Well, at last I have made my husband over." I thought that was quite an achievement. She explained, "He was the gloomiest, most negative man you ever saw. If he wanted something to happen, he thought the way to make it happen was to say it wouldn't happen. Then he would be surprised and pleased if it did happen.

For example," she continued, "he was a great fan of the New York Yankees. He just loved them. When he wanted to be absolutely sure the Yankees would win, he would go around saying they were not going to win. He always thought that would make them win." It's pathetic, isn't it? But many people are like that.

"Every day," the lady continued, "when my husband came down to breakfast, his first words would be, 'This is going to be another lousy day.'"

I suppose that was designed to inspire her and lift her spirits. She went on to tell how her husband would read the newspaper at breakfast and, over each news item, he would say, "Look at that; it is just what I told you. This country is going to the devil."

One morning, as this man was sitting there regaling his wife with how terrible everything was going to be, she turned on the radio and a speaker came on whose voice was filled with vim, vigor, and vivacity. And he said, "Good morning, folks, good morning. I hope you are all feeling bright and happy today."

The husband growled, "Turn that annoying guy off."

But she quietly responded, "Maybe you need to listen to someone like him." And she left on the radio.

What program it was, I wouldn't know, but it was religious in content. By and by, the speaker began to bear down with irresistible logic on the point that if a person would start the day with Jesus Christ, He would fill it full of meaning and vigor and faith and victory over suffering and pain. Finally the speaker concluded by saying, "Please repeat after me one of the great texts from God's Book." And this was the text he gave: "This is the day which the

Lord hath made; we will rejoice and be glad in it."

The woman said to her husband, "You and I are going to pray." She took him by the hand and they prayed together. He was a fine man, she assured me, and he had achieved many things in spite of his negative attitude. And she made him agree that they would predicate that day on the passage of Scripture they had just heard. When the day was over, she told me, even he had to admit it had made the day a good one. "Now," she said, "we start every day by repeating that same passage."

I have gone up and down the country telling people in many places that, if they will say that passage a half-dozen times a day, it will change their lives. And I have had literally scores of people tell me they have done it and have had that kind of result. "This is the day which the Lord hath made." Say that the first thing in the morning, and continue with, "We will rejoice and be glad in it."

If you start a day believing in the best, believing in God's goodness, loving people, being thankful for the work you have to do, and being glad you are alive, you will for sure find goodness in that day. Let me quote a few paragraphs from an article written by a businessman:

> Commencing last October, I started a procedure of saying a brief prayer each morning after arriving at my office and looking at my schedule for the day. I pray to God that I may be calm and orderly in my thinking, putting first things first and acting with confidence and enthusiasm. I pray, that in making each decision, I may act as closely as possible as Jesus Christ would in similar circumstances. I pray for each client whom I am going to write or see. I pray that I may understand them and

that they will understand me, and that we can merge our hearts and minds to the best interest of their families or their businesses.

I have followed this custom for several months, and I can truly say it has greatly increased my capacity for service. I seem to be able to do twice as much work each day with half the nervous tension. I have greater confidence and greater happiness.

Two or three times in the bustle and confusion of the office, I have forgotten to talk with God in this manner. Later in the day, it suddenly came upon me that something was missing, as if I had forgotten to have breakfast. And I quickly returned to my desk and opened my heart to God. After that, all was well. I know that this has brought me closer to God. I feel certain that it is helping me to be a better Christian. And I think I can see in the eyes of my family and my friends and my associates that it is helping them, too.

There was a time when anything like that would have been thought impractical. But in this enlightened day, we are learning that the way for a person to be efficient and effective is to live with God. The writer of this article is a modern businessman. Anyone who says you can't mix religion with business should sell his car and get himself a horse and buggy, for he is completely out-of-date.

The Pittsburgh Experiment in Pittsburgh, Pa., is a wonderful testimony to the power of Christian faith in modern business. Throughout the city, businessmen and women sit down together at luncheon meetings, breakfast gatherings, dinner meetings, and so on, and they bring the bedrock of their faith to the ethical decisions of their work. They pray together about the choices they must make. They depend upon God's guidance and they find it. They know that their faith and their work are not separate. This practice is making successes out of men and women who were struggling in their business life.

So, the first thing about making a day a good one is to start it right. Then, after you have it started right, bring to the day, from hour to hour, those qualities that will keep it good. And what are they? Thinking, human kindness, energy, and love.

Keep alive to the beauty and magnificence and romance in the human experience, and the wonder and the delight of life. When Ramsay MacDonald, onetime Prime Minister of Great Britain, was sitting by the bedside of his wife as she was dying, she said to him, "Ramsay, put romance into the lives of our children. Teach them to see the beauty, the charm and the fascination, the indescribable wonder of the world."

There is so much beauty, so much wonderment all about us, and yet some people seem so insensitive to it. Recently, I was on the West Coast and I flew back to New York City in a large jet. We passed over the Grand Canyon at sunset. I have always wanted to see the Grand Canyon from the air but, every other time I have flown over it, it has been foggy. This time it wasn't. There was the setting sun falling against those enormous pinnacles in all their varied color. As we gazed at the spectacle in utter fascination, a man next to me said, "Even though they have shrunk up the country to four hours and thirty minutes, coast-to-coast, it still is a magnificent land."

But do you know something? There were two or three of my fellow passengers who were sound asleep. How in the world can a person be sound asleep at 33,000 feet, going 670 miles an hour over the Grand Canyon at sunset? I suppose those people, when they got home, likely said to their families, "I had a terrible day today." Or, "We were an hour late getting started!" Or perhaps, "It's going to be a lousy day tomorrow." But those whose eyes were open experienced romance. I saw it in their eyes. Life is full of zest and romance.

"Well," you say, "we can't all go up and ride around in airplanes all the time to experience this romance and beauty." The day I was describing ended, for me, with a long trip by taxicab from the airport to my home. There was a wind blowing a heavy rain. As the cab waited at a red light, I saw the raindrops dancing like diamonds under a street lamp. I thought, *How beautiful rain is, driven by wind, dancing so happily under a street light.* Sensitivity to the beauty and the wonder of the world is romance that anyone can cultivate. And it will be a potent source of good in your days.

"This is the day which the Lord hath made." Just think of that! The Lord made this day, and He gave it to you and me. So let us rejoice and be glad in it. Let us begin each day with a right beginning, and go through the day with romance in our hearts, and love and deep humanity, and end the day in the consciousness of God's presence. You can train yourself to have a good day every day.

No man can deliver the goods if his heart is heavier than the load. —Frank I. Fletcher

CONCLUSION

Will tomorrow bring an end to our troubled times? Only God knows.

But whatever lies ahead, we can count on God's help. The world can be made a wonderful world for all; but this can be accomplished only by the tremendous healing power of God through Jesus Christ working upon people's souls. Trust in God. Believe in Him in depth, and nourish that belief until you *learn* to trust.

Belief is intellectually based. It involves acceptance of the truth of God in one's thinking. Trust may be defined as belief activated. In this instance, you rest completely on your faith, trusting it to sustain you through any crisis. Whenever you feel overwhelmed, the practice of trust in God brings immense resources to your aid.

When problems confront you, you must not allow your mind to acquiesce in defeat, weakly giving up. What seems impossible one minute becomes, through faith, possible the next. That is always the way of it. No one is going to be immune from having problems. So, if we desire to live successful lives, we must become truly expert in problem solving.

In God We Trust

By reading this book, you have taken the first step. Ask God to guide you as you review what you have learned, and as you faithfully begin to apply those principles in your daily life.

My thoughts and prayers are with you.

A NOTE FROM THE EDITORS

If you enjoyed this inspirational book, you might also enjoy reading *Guideposts*, a monthly magazine filled with true stories of people's adventures in faith.

Guideposts magazine is not sold on the newsstand. It's available by subscription only. And subscribing is easy. All you have to do is write to Guideposts, 39 Seminary Hill Road, Carmel, New York 10512. A year's subscription costs only $11.97 in the United States, $13.97 in Canada, and $15.97 overseas. The Large Print edition, for those with special reading needs, is only $11.97 in the United States, $13.97 in Canada, and $15.97 overseas.

When you subscribe, each month you can count on receiving exciting new evidence of God's presence, His guidance and His limitless love for all of us.